The Black Man Drought

An answer to where all the brothers have gone
and how to get them back

ALSO BY LORRAINE JONELL STEPHENS

Sugarcane Sweet (a Caribbean love story)
Novel available Summer 2016

Lorraine Jonell Stephens

The Black Man Drought
An answer to where all the brothers have gone
and how to get them back

The Black Man Drought.
Lorraine Jonell Stephens

22books
P.O. Box. 17534
Sugarland, TX. 77496

ISBN-13:
978-1434899200

ISBN-10:
1434899209

Printed in the U.S.A

To the glory of GOD for his unique creation

Black Men

...and to the Black man that has my heart

Contents

The Black Man Drought

An answer to where all the brothers have gone
and how to get them back

Why are brothers disappearing? If I knew I'm sure I could make some serious cash because like a tortured man longs for release or like a war torn nation longs for peace there are some sad single sisters out here craving the chocolaty touch of a sexy-fine, devilishly divine, body of a Greek god, oh so gentle man. They're yearning for the companionship of a warm, sensitive, throw back phrase from the nineties "homie-lover-friend" and in desperate need of a reliable, hardworking, strong Black man for support of the kids and the bills.

If I knew where the remaining brothers hid, I'd round them all up, tie them up and sell them. After all we live in a capitalist society and Black men are definitely in high demand so I figure, why not supply. But before I put this testosterone induced product out there on the shelf I'd have to make sure what I have is top of the line merchandise. Part of my shifting process would include putting them through the fire to see what they're really made of and honey, if he isn't tough, ashes to ashes and dust to dust.

A weak man simply won't survive the heat and I'm not only talking about the physically weak. I'm excluding all spiritually weak, namby-pamby, spineless, emotionally disturbed, weak minded males. Lazy, disrespectful, stubborn, self-absorbed liars will also be dismissed and the commitment phobic, I-have-to-have-more-than-one-woman-because-I'm-a-pimp-or-player, or the live-with-you-for-ten-years-never-going-to-marry-you-just-going-to-string-you-along kind of men, well consider him and the like literally discarded into the damaged goods bin.

There must not be any faker shakers in the bunch because see, these have to be the thorough bred, the taking care of business, momma loving (but not a momma's boy), gainfully employed or respectfully looking for employment, I'm-going-to-treat-my-woman-right kind of men. After all isn't that what a good man is? Well, once I have them tried and tested like clumps of coal that are buffed and proofed into sparkly diamonds, they'll be ready to market.

One extra large bottle of Benevolent Black Man®, one million dollars. That would be the going rate. Don't even act like sisters wouldn't be scrimping and saving, neglecting to pay their bills, taking out loans and borrowing money from each other to get their hands on some of this product. After all, how much do we spend on hair weaves, nails, make-up, push-up bras, cosmetic surgery, name brand clothing and heels just so we can look good enough to capture the attention of the cutey in our class, at church, at our job or in the club? With some of the tricks and stunts we women already perform to get and keep a good man, with all of the tricks and stunts we pull to get and hold onto a not so good man, I know for a fact I'd make a killing.

On second thought being a young sister myself who at one point in time struggled to stay afloat in a shrinking pool of available Black men, I know how hard it is out here in the dating world so I would be generous to my fellow females and pass Benevolent Black Man® out for free. After all, almost every Black woman I know has had her share of drama, heartbreak and heartache that by the time she's like, well thirty, she's freaking earned it. I'd distribute Benevolent Black man® out evenly among every sister. Could you imagine living on a planet where every Black woman had her fair share of a loving, toe-curling, soul-stirring relationship? The world would witness the resurrection of a uniquely passionate, sweet beautiful creature full of joy and love beyond this earth's containment.

Unfortunately I don't possess a patent for this kind of product and the sad reality is, even if I did, there simply wouldn't be enough Benevolent Black man® to go around. There'd be a few ladies in the back with out stretched arms only to be turned away empty handed. After homicide, homosexuality, drugs, jail and the Black men's kryptonite, White women, Black women are competing for only a handful of men, some of who know this fact and use it to their full advantage. A lot of us have just accepted the notion of a good man being a scarce commodity and have simply settled for loves substitution instead of the real thing or reduced ourselves to sharing. Despite all of the Sexually Transmitted Diseases being passed around these days and the havoc a bad relationship can impose upon our health, finances and self-esteem too many of us take risks with our hearts and lives because we've convinced ourselves of one miserable conclusion; if we want a Black man we better take what we can get because Black men are disappearing.

In America Black women are asking ourselves, "Why are brothers disappearing?" We question each other because residing at the head of too many households are single Black women, lonely and sometimes lonely with an attitude because their men are jumping ship and migrating by the millions out of their lives and the lives of their children. Forget about fancy figures, senseless consensus or stupid statistics, we don't need surveys or charts to tell us there's a deadbeat dad epidemic in the Black community. Neither do we need numbers to persuade us that an uneven percentage of our men are filling up American correctional facilities. And strolling down the streets sisters can see for themselves that in the lives of more and more Black men the role of leading lady is constantly being given away to White, Asian and Latina women.

Even in the physical presence of too many Black males there's still an absence of sentiment. The emotions are gone, the tenderness, sweetness, that soft spot that lends itself to opening up the core of his soul is replaced with a hard shell built to protect himself from years of emasculation by White America. Outside of anger, little Black boys are taught to hide their feelings because in a world so cold and cruel and especially in a country with a history as dark as the pain that lies within his eyes, a Black male is not allowed to show weakness or vulnerability.

But the most precious aspect of a Black man threatened to the point of extinction is his essence, his soul, his spirit, his ability to relate to, understand and follow spiritual principals and laws for his own benefit and that of the community he is supposed to lead, guide and protect. In most Black churches around America Black women disproportionately fill up the pews, left to worship, praise and sing hallelujah to the Lord without their husbands, sons and fathers along for the spiritual ride. Since I believe the Black man is made in Gods own image and his own likeness, I'm heartbroken to see our most influential earthly representation of the divine fallen from his heavenly place of spiritual leadership only to be replaced with what the current generation proudly flaunts as a materialistic, money hungry, sexually perverted, irresponsible, directionless and oh so lost victim of racism, the Black woman's scorn and his own sins.

I'm fully aware that as the backbone of our society Black women share an equal portion of accountability and responsibility, but the Black man is the leader and the provider. His inability or unwillingness to provide may leave us starved and the paths he chooses to travel may lead us further down than we've already sunk. We need the Black man. We need more loving, honest, strong, faithful, ambitious, responsible hardworking brothers taking care of their kids, their women and themselves, but as it is now its plain to see that a growing portion of our men are disappearing physically, disconnected emotionally and spiritually dying. This is why it was important for me to write this book.

I wanted to know why Black men are disappearing, what exactly is it that's taking them away from us and most importantly not only how can we keep them, but how do we create a supportive environment that nurtures and promotes their desire to stay, survive and strive.

The content in these pages are heavy, yet sensitive and as extreme as they are truthful because the thoughts and opinions expressed are purely my own taken from a collaboration of real life situations and events and the people I've dealt with up close and personal. Instead of watering down my experiences with cold encyclopedia reference or dressing them up with textbook statistics I'm writing about my perception, which is my reality and the reality of other Black women.

The reality is Black women are fighting a battle for their men, sons, husbands, brothers, fathers and their children's fathers. A battle with too much at stake and one we cannot afford to lose. Winning the battle is going to start with confrontation of the crises and confrontation begins with truth. We cannot afford to cover up, bury, sweep underneath the carpet, continue to provide excuses or refuse to tackle the issues. The spiritual tax we've already paid for doing so is simply too high.

So, from the pain, anguish and disappointment I've suffered at the hands of former lovers, friends and acquaintances, through my curious attempts over countless years to unravel the mystery of their actions and most importantly out of love and utmost respect for Black men I give you this book. Enjoy and be enlightened!

– *Lorraine Jonell Stephens*

The Black Man Drought

"Daddy, Where are you?"

I'll hate to see this little girl in a few years, in the arms of some man who is trying to be her father figure because right now she is crying and whining and soaking up her pretty little lacy yellow dress with tears only her daddy can comfort. Through the window she can see hundreds of cars speed by, but not a single one of them will slow down to stop in front of her house. Her mama is in the background pacing back and forth cursing into the air saying, "I knew that no good nigga wasn't gonna show up," full of rage and regret at his broken promises, full of sorrow because she had to witness her daughters first heartbreak.

I say I'll hate to see this little girl in a few years because at three years old she has already learned not to depend on the support and contribution of male figures. She can barely count, but has already learned not to count on the value of promises, the security of covenants or the freedom of trust. For the rest of her childhood and probably throughout her entire life she will be afraid to trust people or she may be too eager to trust, being careless in relationships and with her body, not knowing the full value of her own heart.

Through a personal relationship with God, with positive female and male role models in her life, added to an extra dose of love and a steady stream of positive affirmations about her self worth and beauty baby girl can bounce back. She can grow up to be a confident, self assured, self respecting, happy, healthy woman with a warm heart and a good head on her shoulders, but as it is now the standard she has to measure on what a man is supposed to do, how a man is to behave and how he is supposed to treat a woman, her daddy, is a disappointment.

Every time I see a naive fifteen or sixteen year old waddling around with a big pregnant belly or balancing a book bag on one shoulder and a screaming toddler on the other I wonder if their daddies were disappointments too. More often than not the little fast chicks who some are quick to label as "hoes" are fighting serious self esteem issues and insecurities tied to an inability to gain their fathers affection. Out to win the feel good love and approval denied by daddy they fall into all kinds of heartbreaking traps. They make themselves up, paint their nails, spritz their hair, cover themselves in next to nothing and use their curves in hot pursuit of male attention. The classic *I'm hurt and I need love* scream cleverly disguised with a sassy attitude, skimpy skirt and an award winning performance meant to hide the reality of rape, molestation and abandonment.

Sweet little girls who lack love and attention from their daddies or a healthy example of a male-female relationship all too many times grow up with dangerously distorted views of their sexuality. They open their hearts and their legs like a free buffet for the first smooth talking man who comes along and shows them some attention to take as much as he wants.

And their knuckle head counterparts who run wild, untamed and socially untrained with sagging pants literally sliding off of their boney butts, holding their sacks in one hand thinking they are holding onto their manhood, I wonder who or what is at home feeding this example. I wonder if they can say *my father taught me how to ride a bike and although I fell and scraped up my knees on the cold hard concrete he was always there to pick me up, brush the dirt off my shoulders and encourage me to keep going*; a metaphor for life and a helluva way to inspire determination, perseverance and instill strength in a Black child who will certainly face bumps at every curve in the road. Or is it the common case of *if I knew where the sorry sperm donor was I'd kick his butt for leaving my mama to do some hard mess like take care of my bad tail all by her lonesome.*

Currently twenty million or so butt whippings are sitting on reserve for the deadbeat dads of America, which mean a majority of our children are disregarded, misguided, or simply stumbling through life without a strong male figure to scoop them up when they fall or to straighten them out when in the midst of peer pressure their edges start to roughen.

In the hood what can a little itty-bitty woman say to her child that's going to remain in his head throughout the day to help him resist temptation when his boys are passing freshly wrapped blunts underneath his nose? How is she going to relate the message of self worth, pride or respect to a man who's a product of the streets day to day dealings, an environment structured by confusion where looking at somebody a second too long might end in an emergency room visit and where disrespect means accidentally stepping on somebody's overpriced sneakers, which might also cause a swollen and bloody rush to the E.R.

How is she even going to discipline him if he doesn't listen when he's only fourteen, but already towering over her at six feet tall? He'll start running right over his mom, coming and going as he pleases all while she's crying, pulling her hair out and complaining to other family members that she can't control her child. But what does she expect when his whole life she's labeled him as the man of the house? Because in the absence of his father, he has been expected to step up and fill in that role, protecting his mother, sometimes even stealing or selling drugs to provide and pay the bills if there's no part-time work available in the neighborhood, which there usually isn't. So what is a belt going to do to a child the size of Lebron James who thinks he's the man of the house?

Oh, but let daddy be in the home. Not a drunken daddy or an abusive daddy or an I'm too busy at work or too tired after work to discipline these kids daddy, not those types of fathers, but I'm talking about a regular old school by the book James Evans from *Good Times* daddy. Let that type of daddy be a part of the equation and he won't even think twice about giving into the temptation of the streets. Disrespecting mama won't even enter into his thoughts because daddy has his size 13 work boot ready to shove down his throat if it does. No sir, a teenager isn't the man of the house, an actual man is the man of the house.

Discipline from a male works better on boys than discipline from a woman. It's just biological. There isn't a woman alive who knows what it's like to be a man, or understand why little boys and young men do the things they do and get into all the trouble they get into. Men relate a certain unspoken message that boys naturally adhere to and respect, a message a woman could never express to the same degree or effect. Boys need someone who has felt the same emotions and been tempted with the same temptations to correct their behaviors and show them how to handle themselves in certain situations. Whether it's a warning to watch out for the neighborhood chicken heads or to keep his nose in his school books and out of the dangerous affairs of the streets, young men need their fathers' correction, discipline, and love.

When they don't have it of course they're not doomed for life, plenty of boys have grown up in single parent homes or have grown up without their fathers and still turned out to be wonderful, more than wonderful men, but think of how much more wonderful they could've been if daddy didn't disappear. Parenting isn't a single person sport. A woman didn't crawl on top of herself and get herself pregnant, so why should she play parenting solitaire? A lot of single mothers are doing the best that they can, they have no choice but to do their best, but in a cut throat world sometimes that best just won't cut it.

If more Black men decided to roll their sleeves up and get actively involved in their children's lives instead of selfishly forsaking fatherhood the wanna-be thugs who line the corner of almost every major inner city selling dope, shooting dice and shooting each other would be headed to top universities and higher learning facilities instead of cemeteries and penitentiaries. Because there is no one to point them in a direction other than the wrong one, the sad destiny for too many Black males born in America is an early grave or an orange jumpsuit.

With every murder, rape or robbery they're silently begging, pleading and screaming *daddy, where are you?* the same desperate chant heard in defunct buildings in the ghetto, echoed in the pissy hallways by fiends and addicts. It's sung by struggling single mothers who've gotten no help from their children's father, no education and thus no way out of the same cycle their mothers and grandmothers found themselves in. It's in the wailing at maternity wards where middle school girls are instantly matured into mothers or in the city morgue where another young brother lays slain, cold and toe tagged.

The billions of dollars that have passed through the hands of politicians and legislators for state funded programs, referendums, initiatives and movements and our own Farrakhan lead Million Man march still hasn't been effective or lasting enough to change the station or at least turn down the volume on "Daddy, where are you?" the sad song written and recited by countless Black children.

The common attitude of the generation of girls I came up with was *hey, my mama did it without help from a man and if push comes to shove that's the way I'm gonna to do it, so long as I get that child support check.* Some of the boys held the same attitude thinking just like their own departed daddies that *hey, she don't need my help so why bother* able to totally detach themselves from any responsibility associated with raising the child they fathered.

In high school it became apparent that the rock solid traditional family of the 1960's Civil Rights era where 70% of all Black households were headed by married couples had somehow been shaken and stirred down through the years into a crumbly little mess that made it not only acceptable for our men to abandon their families, run like cowards and vanish never to be heard from, talked about or seen, but for our women to expect and nonchalantly pass it over as the norm.

I would roll my eyes at my Black Puerto-Rican friend, Tammy who had long thick curls she wore on her shoulders and light brown eyes she'd roll right back every time I tried to talk her out of auditioning for the lead role of Single Teenaged Mother. A roll I didn't think she could play very well with no job, no money and at fifteen still living at home with her mother. Posted up by our lockers between classes we would go at it like two high powered attorneys trying to convince the jury of each others flawed points of view.

"Before the year is up I'm going to get pregnant," She would announce as her opening statement, proud and stubborn reminding me of those old psychic ladies from those infomercials who believed for $3.99 a minute they could tell you if your man was cheating, which technical school to enroll in to make you the most coins and the secret to happiness and success. Tammy wore big gold hoop earrings, a gold necklace that spelled her name out in cursive letters and a set of gold bangles that jangled together harmoniously whenever she strutted up and down the hallways. You could always hear Tammy or smell her Designer Imposters body spray way before you'd even see her coming.

"And whoever don't like it just gotta deal with it," She added, neck rolling in coordination with those eyes. Tammy was a real Puerto-Rican mamacita; colorful, bold, loud, spicy attitude in all.

"First of all, you don't have a boyfriend so who is the daddy going to be?" I wondered wanting to know if she planned on having a baby by the invisible man because as far as I knew she wasn't kicking it with anybody or at least anybody I'd ever seen.

Tammy's mouth twisted and eyes floated to the top of her head advertising a puzzled face like she was just as stumped as I was.

"Somebody, anybody, I don't know and I don't care as long as he gives me what I want, a baby, he can bounce," She said and then changed her tune to a casual carefree, "don't no real woman need a man around to raise a baby anyway. As long as a child got one parent around to love them, clothe them and feed them, that's all they need."

"Yeah, but how are *you* going to clothe and feed your soon-to-be baby when you don't even have a doggone diploma or a red cent to your name?" That was the million-dollar question most broke and struggling teenage mothers lived to regret never asking themselves.

"And look at your situation," I said hoping she would open her pretty brown eyes to the reality of her condition. "How can you even think to bring a child into all of that?" No job. No man. No money. Bad grades. Held back in the ninth grade once already and about to flunk out again. Why oh why she felt like complicating matters by having a child struck me as down right dumb. Tammy just didn't fit the profile of someone ready to bring life into this world, let alone sustain that life.

"Look at my situation?" she repeated, then repeated again insulted and in awe that I would even ask such a question. "Look at my situation?" Her neck, hands and animated facial expressions were all in accord working overtime to emphasize the apparent offense she took to my statement. Quick to defend herself and even quicker to set me straight, she laughed a dismissive laugh as if to say I was foolish or didn't know what I was talking about and began to explain how everything was under control and that I should not worry about her *situation* because there really was no situation at all.

Tammy said that while her mom would be disappointed in her decision at first, after the baby was born her family would all be very happy, supportive and willing to help out anyway they could. As far as taking care of the child while she went to school or whenever she needed a break, childcare and daycare expenses were not to be fussed over when her grandma and unemployed older sisters were already live-in babysitters.

The church where she was a member, but admittedly barely ever attended outside of Christmas and Easter services, had recently carved out a special outreach ministry for single parents, donating money, offering childcare, and parenting classes for new mothers and pregnant girls in need. The rest (whatever welfare and the government didn't cover) including toys, clothes, bottles, bibs, cribs all of that would come hand-me-down from her sisters, cousins and aunties who had a bunch of kids themselves, along with plenty of advice, plenty of help and enough family around for the baby to overdose or at least get high off of love.

It was crystal clear that a tight family, as Tammy believed, not only contained the power to thin out any *'situation'*, but also created a soft comfortable cushion protecting her from the consequences of her actions. I asked, "But what about the baby's daddy?"

"What about him?" She asked back just as cool and as relaxed as if I'd questioned her about a carton of eggs she forgot to pick up from the grocery store or about a missing sock from the drawer. It seemed strange to me how someone who held her family in such high regards with thoroughly thought out details for their roles in her child's life would fail to acknowledge the importance of the father or the part he played in it.

"Whoever he is, I know you said he can bounce on out after the baby is born, but what if he doesn't? What if he decides to stick around? After all it's his child too. Have you thought about what it's going to be like between the two of you?"

With her pretty brown eyes she said, "tell me girl, how many of the boys you know actually stick around? They don't stick around, they gone as soon as they bust a nut." Tammy snickered, "It'll be hard enough to track him down to even tell him I'm pregnant, so dealing with him is the least of my concerns."

"My point exactly," I shot back. "Why would you have a baby knowing the daddy isn't going to be around?"

"Because," she whined, growing more irritated by the minute. She let her hand rest on her hip and the set of gold bangles slid down her arm clanking together as if they too were irritated. "This is my decision, my body, my aching feet, my swollen ankles, my morning sickness, my fat giggly booty that's gonna be carrying around all *my* extra baby weight and he sure as hell ain't gonna help me push. So," She hardened her voice into a stern no nonsense tone, "this is my baby, I won't need him."

"But *your* baby will," I said and fiddled with the combination to my locker. I thought, *why make a baby if you're not planning to give the baby your all, your everything and the absolute best?* No doubt that included a father. I said, "Don't you want to wait until you're old enough to know what you're doing, until you're safe, paid and married to a man that's not going to just up and jump out the bed and out the door after the do is did?"

Tammy shrugged her sharp boney shoulders in a way that told me she didn't care, a defiance indicating she wasn't connecting to my words or grasping onto my logic, wanting what she wanted under her terms and conditions made her too blinded by selfishness to look at things from a another set of eyes. I tried to flip the script to see it from her perspective, but to me a baby minus an education, minus money and minus a husband equaled nothing but stress, struggle and a hard life. It just didn't add up to making sense. I placed my hand on my hip as well and sucked my teeth just like a fed up mother who was at her wits end with her unruly child. The battle going on inside my head over what might be going on in Tammy's baffled me. "Girl, you're only fifteen years old, you should be scarred out your holy drawers."

Young, naïve and ignorant to what a crash course in life, a few months experience and a few sleepless nights with a bawling baby would eventually teach, she innocently, naively and ignorantly asked, "Scarred for what?"

It only took a second for me to collect my notebooks and textbooks from my locker, turn my back on Tammy as I shook my head in frustration, blow a tired aggravated breath and wave her off, "I'll see you at lunch, girl."

"Wait up," I heard her call out while I made a quick swerve around the corner on my way to class. A big fake Gucci purse and a tote that held her books lunged around her shoulders and attached to her hip like a Siamese twin bouncing up and down as she skipped to catch up with me. "I hear what you're saying and all, but I ain't afraid because trust me, lots of girls before me did it with or without a boy by their side. Broke, beat up, beat down, at fifteen or at forty--my mom did it, her mom did it and her mom before her did it, and did it so gracefully they should've all won Lifetime Achievement Awards, but they did it without even a pat on their backs because Black women, we bad like that and we can do it like that."

"So," she said after a long sigh, "the earth won't stop rotating nor will the sun fail to rise just because I have a damn baby. Damn." "And if it does," she added, "then I'm still willing to risk it to have something cute and cuddly to hold and to call my own." Her defensive demeanor turned soft and starry eyed as her arms became cradles pretending to rock an imaginary newborn inside of them and while she drifted away into baby la-la land I knew right then and there that I wouldn't be able to turn her off to what her environment, her upbringing and society had taught her to be no big deal.

The, "I want something cute and cuddly to hold" from Tammy's defense seemed like a shallow alternative to confessing she simply wanted and needed something to love her. She wouldn't admit it, but having a baby just seemed like the easiest way for a girl with limited resources, skills and options to obtain the love and affection withheld by her parents, daddy especially. Finding true love among the neighborhood hustlers, players or regular immature clowns who delighted in lying their way into as many panties as possible proved as tiresome and as pointless as running up a muddy hill in four inch Christian Louboutins. Expecting to mold them into faithful and committed husbands, a straight up dumb thought better left to fairytales and daydreams.

Instead of investing precious years waiting on Prince Charming to come sweep them off their pretty little pedicured feet, then becoming bitter and angry when he never showed up, getting pregnant took much less time and even less effort with an adorable baby to love and give love as the payoff. This is how most love starved females reasoned failing to realize that babies are selfish, dependent and need a lot more love than he or she can offer and that having the daddy around was better for all parties involved. Having a loving relationship with the daddy, even better, like the light fluffy whipped cream icing to top off the cake, but girls like this you couldn't tell them anything.

Before graduating from High school Tammy's story lost its shock value as I would sit across the lunch table or ride the bus with a bunch of chicks who thought, felt and believed just like she did, that they were strong and independent for having and raising their babies by themselves. Only deep down inside they were young, naïve, and empty, using their babies like toy dolls to dress up, play with and show off, like tiny little trophies to fill their lives with some kind of worth and significance.

This is the generation I grew up with, but thankfully survived through, witnessing along the way many more up close and detailed accounts of the screwed up mindsets and ideas and beliefs they held on sex, relationships and parenting. After high school I saw more casualties of the conflict going on in our community between Black men and Black women in the form of illegitimate children with no reason for being born into this world other than their parent's lust and irresponsibility or pure casual attitudes, casual in the sense that being married to the mother or father of their child no longer mattered, neither did sharing an exclusive loving and committed partnership.

Casual in the sense that if the child's skin happened to come out slightly lighter or darker than the daddy's he questioned and quickly denied responsibility and when confronting the mother, finding the real father became a guessing game of potentially two, three or four different men lined up for paternity tests.

Casual in the sense that despite every sociological study, examination, investigation, analysis, researched report or statistic inundated with proof that children in stable two parent homes have higher self esteem, are better adjusted, have less learning disabilities, are less likely to drop out of school, are less likely to end up in juvenile or jail or prison, etcetera-etcetera-etcetera our people still have coined and glorified terms like Baby Daddy and Baby Momma kicking honorable titles of Husband and Wife on over to the side.

Casual in the sense that the sad irony of it all is what was once disgraceful; our broken homes, our makeshift families and our unplanned pregnancies, have now become a kick back on the couch, put your feet up, grab the remote control, popcorn and soda affair. Entertainment. Episodes of silly daytime talk shows air out our dirtiest laundry over the laugh and applause of millions. Our tragedies are carelessly dismissed as comedy and with a click of a button can just as easily be switched off.

But while the rest of the world is flipping the channel ignorant to the fragile state of Black America, there's a gigantic waving flag we cannot ignore that's been perched up in every Black neighborhood around America indicating the devil has surely declared war on our community, a battle of the sexes where our lack of education and wisdom and especially our gradual migration away from God has left us defenseless in enemy territory.

In our homes, mostly run by women, mothers are forced to fend for themselves doing what they have to do in order to survive the war; sometimes trading in their beauty, morality and sanity for the ugliness, sin and insanity associated with the degrading jobs and acts they are driven to perform to feed their children when a tumbling economy or an unjust legal system or drug dependency or pure irresponsibility has crippled our men.

Some of us threw our hands up in surrender when they killed

off the strong, ready, razor sharp warriors of yesterday. Our Martin's and Malcolm's and our Medgar Evans' who armed with the brass knuckles of self knowledge, discipline, and an uncompromising faith in a greater destiny and love for Black people fought for our integrity, whipped some tail for our freedom and with an army of mad guerillas trekked through the cold concrete jungles of America to conquer injustice. These unintentional soldiers placed themselves in harms way because they knew if not them who else would fight for our honor.

In the good old days when the majority of families were still intact, before the pimp of pop culture prostituted our souls demanding that we bow before idols; worship money and material, praise ice, big butts, and name brand clothes, these men stood and many times died for the Lord, us and the cause. It was better that they breathe their last breath marching through Alabama than to hide behind the window curtains and from the safety of their homes watch the people they were supposed to be leading be lead astray. They were men in every sense of the word, devoted, dependable, tough, masculine, confident, big, bold fearless Black men, not cocky, self centered, arrogant, weak, irresponsible, spoiled mama's boys. We thank God for our modern day heroes, but we'll forever mourn the loss of our chivalrous black knights, yesterday's fighters.

Today many of our castles are kingless so we throw on our soldier rags, our dainty hands and knobby knees all scraped up and ashy out there on the battle ground trying to support and applaud the few good ones who are willing to fight, while still managing to hold on tight to the little sanity we have left from watching all the others scatter and flee like roaches when the lights turn on. When the well-off brothers are nestled snug with White women and all the others are unemployed and broke, strung out on drugs, psychologically screwed up or from a variety of reasons simply gone, the Black woman is left behind to lose the war because alone she can't win. But even more disturbing than the supposed leaders of our community running and hiding from responsibility leaving their women to lace up our boot straps, buckle up our belts to take charge and fill in the vacant spaces they've created, is the lies, the excuses and the stories some of them conjure up in order to convince us, the world and even themselves that they share none of the blame.

Enlightening me on the reality of how too many of our men will whip out their finely crafted brushes and paint themselves with a glossy coat of victimization, the injured party of selfish and scorned women was Dwayne. This laid back, smooth talking little boy playing dress up pretending to be a man pulled out a chair and offered me a front row seat to view the childish haphazard handling of fatherhood by a young brother choosing to bob and weave from responsibility instead of fight to handle his business like a man. This was the first scene in a series of poorly produced dramas I would witness from my Black brothers, but sadly not the last.

I'd gotten all cute; lipstick, hair, French tipped nails, everything was on point. Grabbed my chocolate brown leather coat meant for wrapping around my slinky pink dress and strutted out the door to be picked up one chilly Friday night. Good food, a good movie, and a good looking man meant a real date and a real good time.

A few weeks earlier we met at one of Houston's hotspots, a jumping little club in midtown called Vibrations and after sweating and moving to each other's rhythm practically the whole night we exchanged numbers. On the phone without hesitation we immediately ran background reports verifying that the other was sane and sound-minded. After all the club scene is crawling with deceivers and liars; people who front like the Jag being dropped off at the valet is theirs instead of their mama's or the knockoff purse around their shoulder came from Prada or Louis Vuitton or Christian Dior and not the $19.99 knock off beauty supply store bin.

Even worst is the crop of not so gentlemen who'll buy you a drink, seduce you with good conversation, a stream of compliments and an impressive resume only to discover the big secret camouflaged behind their sexy smiles the second after fluids have been swapped. The big secret being he's a brother on the down low, or a pathological liar, or a woman beater, or an addict, or crazy and possessive, or straight up married. Everyone wears a mask so before I let my heart slip and slide into this cute strangers care I investigated.

"You in school?" That was the first question on my list because although going to college didn't mean you possessed a pure heart or even a good head on your shoulders for that matter, it's a whole lot of fools in school, education in some form or fashion definitely upped a brothers ante.

"I'm a student at San Jacinto Junior college, but I'm not going to front. I'm sitting the semester out on academic suspension so I'm just slaving a full time job right now, you know."

"Academic suspension?" I repeated coolly making sure not to

turn my nose up because I was in community college myself and my grades weren't all that great either. Another D or F and I'd be sitting right next to Dwayne, suspended from school for a semester. I let him know about my plans to transfer to a local university, my intended major, my age and my last name along with all that other boring stuff men need to know just so they can say they know something about you other than your bra size. And just in case people asked about this fine man I'd be strolling around town with I continued the questions so I could have something to report on.

"What about your family? Where's mama and them?" I asked with a down home southern drawl.

"Mama and them," He chuckled, repeating with a certified Texas accent to rival mine, thick and syrupy sweet like homemade peach cobbler. "Well, mama is here in Houston and the rest of *them* are in St. Croix, Virgin Islands. Some of my people are over there, some of them over here, but the majority of them are over there. I'm an Island boy," He announced proudly proclaiming his West Indian roots.

Covering the mouthpiece with the palm of my hand I whispered, *"Island men are sexy"* and smiled ear to ear. Inside I glowed with intrigue at the picture of exotic fruits stemming from palm trees dancing in the wind, white sandy beaches glistening underneath a tangerine sun, endless emerald mountains swallowed by low powder puff clouds and it all enhanced by the sexy seduction of sweet reggae music. My cheesy smile upgraded to a devilish grin at the possibility of my new friend being as mysteriously captivating as his island.

"What did you say?" Dwayne's heavy voice broke into my thoughts. Two more minutes and I would've been lying on a warm blanket of sand making imaginary love to him on the beach. I caught myself for a moment "Oh, I said, s*o you're from the islands. That's nice."*

"Yeah mon," He said this time switching his southern peach cobbler to a spicy West Indian chicken curry, mixing another chuckle in with my giggle.

"That's cool," I said keeping my excitement level tightly sealed suppressing any hint of attraction. Although he'd already stroked a spark of interest, for a pretty young thang wrapped together in a dangerous combination of beauty and brains like me, he'd have to work a little harder to ignite the fire.

I asked, "So, how old were you when you came to the states?"

"Aw, I was just a lil' man," He answered. "My only memory of the day we left is stepping off the plane and bawling my eyes out because the cold weather was burning my face. November in New York is like a meat freezer."

"Cold?"

"Ice cold." He blew a frosty old man winter breath through the phone receiver, the kind of exhale that would fog up somebody's window and explained how his first taste of America was a housing project in Brooklyn. That's where he spent the majority of his life before trailing down south to chase the heat and the humidity of the Lone Star state.

"Back then I couldn't understand why we left our breezy mango colored crib in the tropics to live in a cold, cramped, roach invested apartment in the 'hood," He said taking me along with him on a trip down memory lane. "Those first couple years were hard. It was just me and my moms and she would walk me to school everyday because she was scared somebody would snatch me away if I walked by myself."

I laughed imagining how cute he must've been as a little boy.

"I mean we did live in the projects so moms was always watching her back and watching the hell out of mines, but do you know how embarrassing it is to be the only kid in the neighborhood still being walked to school in junior high?" We both shared a laugh on that one and I wondering about this crazy overprotective woman who carried this man around in her belly for nine months. His first love that gave up half her DNA, her figure and her freedom so he could live comfortably and be safe.

"You and your mom must be close then, huh?" I asked.

"Most definitely," He said with total confidence in their bond. "She's the number one woman in my life. Any female I meet has got to know my moms comes first."

I could respect that. They say the best predictor of how a man is going to treat his woman is how he treats his mama so nothing was sweeter than listening to him praise and pay homage to his mama.

That night on the phone I got the chance to hear more about his past experiences, stories, opinions and philosophies on life and was respectfully granted the opportunity to voice mines, which stirred up a decent little conversation lasting for hours. We went toe to toe with outrageous tales of crazy family members, past relationships and basically what we stood for and wouldn't stand for and after opening up to me on a very personal level he left me giddy, down right dripping in anticipation to peel off my layers and unveil more of the real me. From all sounds he seemed like a pretty cool guy, decent, down to earth, smart, funny, all of that good stuff and the chemistry brewing between us, unmistakable.

So there I was, secure that I knew enough about him to do the one-on-one thing, a night out alone in the city with a man I'd just met, no double dates, group outings or one of my girls as back up, just the two of us. Dwayne rolled up in a clean deep navy blue Escalade sitting on at least 20 inches of pure chrome rims and met me outside the gate of my apartments. A, y*ou look better than I remember* smile immediately spread ear to ear on his face when his eyes peeked underneath my coat and absorbed the frosty pink colors of my dress lying sleek over my curvy body. The club was smoky and dark the night we met so I was pleased he'd gotten this second chance to see me in the light and was happy with what he saw. Playing the part of a perfect gentleman he opened the passenger side door and gently guided me into his big blue truck as if I were a black porcelain doll able to break at the slightest stroke of roughness.

As I fastened my seat belt and watched him through the window cool and confidently swing around to the drivers seat with the Black man's *I-got-the-world-wrapped-around-my-nuts* strut I couldn't help but showcase the same smile. He stood NBA player tall and thin, but not too thin, he was still strapping the way I like my men to be with shoulders as broad as a linebackers. Preppy and dapper in a solid black blazer over a fresh white tee and crisp dark jeans covering long lean legs that were surely underneath. Rocking a black, red and white 59fifty Yankees cap with the gold sticker on it and a pair of white on white Nikes. His skin, resembling freshly whipped peanut butter was clean-shaven, even toned, smooth, and clear like he'd been swept straight from the pages of Black Men's magazine. I was feeling his East coast swag.

When he sat down and settled into the tan leather seats which stylishly complimented the wood grain that made up the whole interior of his truck, his scent I quickly recognized. It matched his look. It matched the grown and sexy sophistication of the evening. The lady-killer. Armani Code. His blue sapphire truck zoomed off leaving the apartment complex and all my uncertainty behind as I sat back soaking up the aroma until I was completely lost in the lust his flavor created.

We hit the hectic Friday night traffic along with the cracks and potholes of Houston's Westheimer strip, but his certified star status truck stayed virtually unaffected. It didn't matter if horns were being pressed on all around us because even with the windows rolled down, if I shut my eyes I could've sworn we were lounging on a yacht in the middle of the Pacific riding a steady wave. That's how smooth his ride was.

"So, what's up for tonight?" I asked although it didn't matter because wherever we went I just wanted to be seen in this ride with this sexy man by my side.

Without missing a beat, taking his eyes off of the road or anything he smirked like it was nothing, "first I gotta drop my son off at my mom's house." I sat up. Hold up, wait a minute. If I was driving I would've been smashing on the breaks right about now. "Son," I repeated, mouth flying open and staying open as if I'd just tasted the tartness of a sour lemon or bitten into a fiery jalapeño pepper.

"Yeah, my son," He said and my eyes followed his to the back seat where a beautiful brown baby was bundled into a car seat and fast asleep. Quiet. So quiet I wondered if he was even alive underneath the blue blanket someone had wrapped him up in. When my eyes met back up with Dwayne's I couldn't even hide the shock, the bewilderment or the *where the hell did he come from* gaze holding my expression hostage. I tried to force a smile, but he'd already seen right through it and began apologizing over and over again. "Don't worry baby girl, I really want to take you out somewhere nice tonight and I'm not gonna let nothing stop that so you be cool, aight."

Son? My emotions sizzled, a million thoughts bounced around the car like popcorn in a heated pan making my head swell with confusion. About to pop and on the edge of my seat I reached into my little cotton candy pink purse, the one that matched the dress I was rocking, but I couldn't remember why or what I was looking for.

"Son?"

Out the corner of my eye I could see his eyes moving back and forth dividing his concentration between me and the road.

"You mad?" He asked obviously already knowing the answer. What a dumb question, who wouldn't be? A baby magically appears out of thin air like a magician pulling a rabbit out of a hat. *Surprise I'm a daddy.* Never any mention of a baby mama, never any mention of his relationship with her? Did he have a baby mama or was she his wife and was he hiding a marriage from me too? After hours and hours of conversation over the phone talking about everything under the sun if he could conveniently forget to mention he had a child what else could he have conveniently forgotten to tell me? My screwed up face, wretched and vexed stare gave him an obvious answer.

"You so sexy when you get mad," Dwayne said licking his thick pink lips as if he could sweet talk himself out of my anger. "I could pull this car over right now and we could do some things. Sexy ass." He lifted an eyebrow and winked, *you know what I mean.* Pretty boys always thought they could cast a spell over a woman with a few fancy words, make her forget she was mad with promises of *I'll make it up to you,* calm her down with fake sugary compliments but me, I wasn't having it.

"Ain't in the mood for jokes," I said stiffly, cold. Moving slowly over each word and getting loud on him. A few cuss words followed. The roar in my voice made him relax on those funny comments. He got serious again.

"Don't be mad. I know I should've told you about him, but I didn't think it was that big a deal."

"Not that big a deal." Repeating those very words left a bad taste in my mouth. My mouth felt hot and dry, the most arid region of the most barren land. Now I remembered the cool mint in my purse and popped it sucking hard until it completely dissolved on my tongue.

"Have you lost your damn mind? If a baby isn't a big deal to you, then what the hell is?"

"I'm not saying *he's* not a big deal," Dwayne said honking his horn at a car swerving in and out of traffic cutting him off. "I'm just try'na say *it's* not a big deal."

"Boy, that's what you just said, isn't that what you just said or am *I* the one losing my mind?" Again my eyes roamed to the back seat for a second glance of the baby or maybe to see if he was really there and not just a trick of my silly imagination. I blinked, but the baby didn't disappear. The sweet little thing looked so new, no more than a few months old I guessed and as small as a pack of brown sugar with a sweet caramel skin tone many shades lighter than his papa, but definitely a living, breathing carbon copy of Dwayne. Under a different set of circumstances my heart would've been melting butter, as soft and as wide eyed as cutie pie's, but I could do nothing but frown at the baby.

"Tell me," I said talking through angry gritted teeth, yet my tone was a little more relaxed thinking maybe I could reason with him and get some answers if I was calm. "Why didn't you just tell me you had a child from the jump?"

My question was left hanging in the air because he pulled his eyes away from the other fanatical Friday night drivers hogging up the street to follow the sound of a catchy rap tune coming from a cell phone somewhere hidden in the car. Saved by the ring tone. When he found it wedged underneath his seat cushion he squinted his eyes checking the caller I.D. and smiling as if he'd been let off the hook, "What'sup?"

The person on the other end must've been somebody special. His voice quieted almost to a whisper, so soft and so low, and so sexy. Flirty even. His responses to whatever the person was running off at the mouth about were short. "Oh forreal...word...that's what it is...not right now...no doubt...okay...cool," like he couldn't carry on a real conversation and say whatever it is he really wanted to say while I was in the car. I could put two and two together. I'm not dumb. I figured it must be some chick.

"Excuse me," I snapped regaining his attention, "you got nerve sitting up here in my face chit-chatting with another girl." Not like I was his girl or anything, but the disrespect of accepting a call from another female while we were twisted up in a heated discussion had me ready to soar through the sun roof of his big beautiful blue truck. Dwayne's body jerked to the abrasive firmness of my voice like a train coming to a screeching halt, breaking up his conversation with what's her name, whoever *she* was.

"Let me hit you back," I heard him say into the receiver rushing off the phone. His thumb mashed the button, then he clipped the cute little Samsung to the sun visor. He reached for my arm, attempted to give a one hand massage and caress my shoulders as a peace gesture, but pissed off I shrugged him off. He became the toxic man and I was running from infection. I didn't want to be touched, rubbed, bothered, nothing.

"Please, just take me home," I said.

"No," he whined hitting a desperate falsetto, the kind of pitch little kids make when they don't want to go to bed or when they refuse to eat their vegetables. When he should've been focusing on the road instead his eyes slid to my chest, mentally massaging my breast through my dress and outlining the contours of my body like a salivating dog with his tongue hanging out.

"You look too damn good for me to take home. I really don't

want to take you home. We didn't even get nothing popping off yet, the night just started."

"Well, now it's ending."

"Come on," He whined again.

"Take me home now," I demanded. My folded arms and sinking bottom lip spoke loud and clear that if he didn't turn this truck around a temper tantrum I'd be a-having.

"Here's what we'll do, alright," Dwayne leaned over to me, let one arm relax on the middle arm rest while the other still steered the wheel, hunched in close like a Football coach huddling together his players for the last play of the game, but I was onto his game and his game was weak. "Let's drop lil' man off, grab something to eat at this lil' Jamaican spot that got a live reggae band on Friday nights, and then we'll go somewhere quiet, you know somewhere laid back so me and you can just talk and chill."

"We don't have nothing to talk about," I said dryly.

"I want to get to know you better."

"Boy please," I said dismissing him with the ghetto girl neck roll, "you know enough about me. You're the one with all the surprises. I need to be digging and finding out more about you."

"I'm like a open book. You can ask me anything. I don't have nothing to hide," he actually had the nerve to say with a straight face.

"I *don't* have nothing to hide. Not no more," Dwayne added after reading the *yeah right* expression plastered all over my face.

"Okay, so answer my question," I said bringing the conversation right back where I needed it to be, on the baby in the back seat and why Dwayne never felt the need to mention he had a child in the first place.

"What question?" He asked.

I gave him a look that said he knew what I was talking about. The look he gave me back told me he did.

He said, "You want the truth?"

I said, "Nah, I want you to lie to me."

He smirked at my sarcasm, "I'll be real with you."

Attitude on full blast, arms still folded, but my ears were wide open. "I'm listening."

I inhaled, held my breath waiting for an explanation. Sucked up some of the air trapped inside the car, caught another whiff of the smell good cologne he'd dipped himself in. Sucked up some more of the air in the car, this time pine cones and peppermint traveled through my nose and made its way deep into my lungs. A green Christmas tree air freshener dangled on the rear view mirror.

He sighed and exhaled slowly lifting a deep breath off of his chest. Like a sinner brought to his knees by the burden of his sins, ready to plead guilty, confess and possibly even beg for forgiveness. Unwilling to make direct eye contact with me he drove and fondled the Christmas tree while he talked.

"In all honestly, I really didn't think it was a big deal. I barely even see the baby. I ain't even sure he even mine. His moms be tripping. I'm just doing her a favor watching him right now, but I'm 'bout to drop him off at my moms house so I can take you out, so you be cool, alright."

I couldn't believe what I was hearing. Was he serious? I rest my palm on my forehead, letting it be my support for an incoming headache and shook my achy head in pity.

"Lair. You hid this from me deliberately and why? You have a child so what, a lot of men have children. Hell, most of ya'll have children. I would've dealt with it and gotten over it, but this I can't get over this." I shook my head. "We just started getting to know each other, we're not far enough along in the game for this kind of deception."

"I realize that," He said.

"Hiding something as important as having a child destroys relationships and we're not even in one," I added.

Dwayne lowered his head in shame, apologized with somber eyes "Look, I'm stupid. I'm dumb and I don't know what I was thinking."

"Or not thinking," I said.

"Or not thinking," He repeated. "But I do want you to know I'm truly sorry."

Dwayne was trying his damnedest to balance concentrating on the road and on easing my apprehension, but was failing miserably at both. The tires burned rubber as he slammed on the brakes causing us to come to a swift halt at a red traffic light. Papers, baby paraphernalia and other junk from the backseat flew or rolled to the front.

My heart fell into the pit of my stomach. I grabbed onto the dashboard for support and to regain myself.

"Will you be careful, you do have a baby on board or did you forget again?" I said catching my breath thankful for the person who invented seat belts. Instinct instantly caused my head to swerve to the back to check up on the little one, but sure enough besides a few gurgles and murmurs he slept on as before.

Dwayne swung his head around to the back as if he did forget and seeing that the baby was okay he regained control of the truck by gripping the wheel extra tight until his knuckles cracked.

"My bad," He apologized to us and cursed himself for driving recklessly, then cursed the stop light for sneaking up on him out of nowhere. We made a right, then another right over a speed bump leading us into a not so nice neighborhood somewhere in a run down part of town many miles away from my usual runnings. Rolling around in a fancy ride in an unfamiliar neighborhood gave me a serious case of the chills, a severe edgy uneasy feeling.

"This don't look like my area, didn't I say take me home?" I asked masking my nerves with attitude, but he kept on driving as if my will or my attitude didn't faze him. He told me we were on our way to his momma's apartment to drop off his son. I informed him he could do serious time for kidnapping, that all I wanted was to be driven home, and just because I was a petite thing don't let my weight or height fool him because I could very much well do a Jackie Chan move and break every bone in his body without breaking a nail or a sweat if he didn't make a u-turn back to my apartment. I wasn't trying to be funny either, but he laughed at my ranting, called me crazy and told me to relax before I give myself a panic attack.

"Trust me," he said and winked. "Everything is going to be cool."

I sighed feeling indifferent realizing I had no control over the situation. We were now on his playground, under his mercy. He owned the car and the keys and even if I could escape, I didn't know where the hell we were so, "I can't believe this," I finally said and relaxed back carefully watching my surroundings. The access gate to his momma's apartment complex was broken allowing us to drive right on in and over more yellow speed bumps. He parked the SUV in an empty space in front of one of the units, jumped out leaving the car to purr from the key still dangling in the ignition and unbuckled the baby from the car seat in the back.

"This ain't gonna take but a minute," He said and walked up a set of concrete stairs, disappearing behind an apartment door on the second floor.

Not wanting to be a car jacking victim I used the controls on the passenger side panel to roll the windows up and the adjacent controls to lock myself in and everything else out.

He left the high tech very expensive looking system on to bump hip-hop jams I liked, but wasn't in the mood to listen to so I pressed a few buttons on his music player until something soft poured out of the speakers filling up the inside of his ride with velvety instruments; the flute, saxophone, delicate strokes of the piano with Maxwell's voice over them in almost in a whisper telling me about a Woman's Worth.

Five minutes later I'd slightly tilted the seat back to a relaxed position letting the music mellow my mood and soothe my anger into submission. Tonight, I decided would be the last time I spoke to or saw Dwayne and even if I had to grit my teeth to get through what was left of the date I'd do just that, lose his number, then change mine. My confession is his sexy smooth skin, no nasty razor bumps, bruises, pimples or scars, his sleepy almond shaped eyes, thick beautiful lips and the sexy way he licked them moist made my knees buckle. Dwayne had it going on in the looks department, but sexy is on every corner, intersection, cross section, highway and byway. Every woman knows you don't have to search far for an attractive man, you just stumble upon him every so often. The work is in finding the beauty with the brains, the sexiness paired with the humility or the built body accompanied by an honest character, which Dwayne obviously didn't possess.

When he got back in the truck he slammed the door extra hard causing the window to vibrate almost to the point of shattering, but lucky for him it didn't. The sleeves of his blazer were now slightly rolled up to his elbows showcasing a set of hairy arms, one of which carried an undeniably expensive watch. After checking the time on his Cartier, then checking the rear view mirror he flashed me a nervous smile behind swift and paranoid movements.

"What's wrong?" I asked noticing he seemed jumpy and tense almost as if he'd just committed a crime and now had the cops hot on his trail. But before Dwayne could even reply a big whopper of a woman with a loud floral print dress flew out of the upstairs apartment I'd just seen him come out of bouncing Dwayne's son on one of her wide hips. Another child, a cute little light skinned girl clenched her dress tightly and clung to her other hip for dear life as she charged towards us.

They drew close to the car and the lady's huge frame took up the whole side of my window blocking out my view of everything behind her. When she ducked down to peek through the tinted window we were now face to face, but I might as well have not been there by the way her eyes slid right pass me and fixed them selves on Dwayne who pretended as if he didn't see the humungous woman carrying his baby.

She pounded on the window to get his attention, pressed her weight against the glass causing the SUV to rock from one side to the other with ease as if it'd been made of feathers.

"No more children," She yelled, "Do you hear me boy? I said no more children."

Startled half to death and shaken out of my comfortable Maxwell moment I sat up and studied the crazy looking lady with the Caribbean accent and the flaming temper who was screaming to the top of her lungs and giving her self an asthma attack.

Dwayne whimpered virtually sinking in his seat, embarrassed. Visibly shaken, he tried to start the truck up, but he couldn't stop trembling long enough to get the keys in the ignition. He brushed her off by refusing to make eye contact giving her as little acknowledgement as possible hoping that she would somehow disappear, but the woman simply would not be ignored.

"Listen to me. I'm not taking care of any more of your children while you go out wining and dining every and anything with a vagina hole."

Her fist came crashing down on the trucks hood and when she lifted it up a clear dent in the shape of her knuckles remained imbedded in the surface. The sound of bending metal got his attention, perked him right up flying out of the truck to assess the damage. He stood at the grill, ran his hand over the area of the dent comparing it to the rest of the exterior and backed his long legs up to view his ride from further away, then over to the side to view it from all angles. A full moon hung in the night sky and its light glistened clean off of the Escalades' blue finish, but got lost on the spot of the dent.

"Look at my baby," Dwayne cried. "Look what you did to my baby."

"This overpriced piece of junk ain't your baby. This is your baby," the woman said gently shaking Dwayne junior.

"That's the problem. You care more about your car than you do your children."

I tightened my coat before opening my door and stepped out of the truck to meet a chilly January night breeze that whipped itself around my shivering body. "Children," I said sweeping my hair out of my face and finger combing it back in place, "what is she talking about, *children?*"

"Yo, just get back in the truck while I sort this thing out, aight," Dwayne ordered, "And momma, we'll talk about this when I get back."

"When you get back," she laughed. "You not getting back from nowhere because you not going nowhere without your damn kids."

"Hold up, wait a minute," I said ready to have fit, "kids, as in more than one?"

"What," the crazy lady said shifting her weight to one side to better balance the baby who was sliding down her hip, "he didn't tell you about all his children?"

In shock I shook my head no.

"Please," she said shaking her head in pity, "that don't surprise me one little bit. It's easy for him to pretend he don't have any because he don't take care of none of them."

"Momma," Dwayne threw his hands up and flailed them around like a two year old trying to get her to stop revealing more info, but she waved him off. "Look, two of his baby mothers gave this boy partial custody so he can spend time with his kids on the weekend, but whenever it's his turn with the kids he bring them over here. Between his car, all them women he run around with and Lord knows what else, he barely got any time or money left for Dwayne Junior," she said gently shaking the baby, "or Shayla here," she said nudging the little light skinned girl beside her, "or his five year old twin girls, Latoya and Latonya."

I gasped for air. "Twins?"

Dwayne's mama rolled her eyes and smirked, "Latoya and Latonya live in New York with they mom. He ain't seen them in over two years now, worst of all he don't even call them."

My eyes widened, a million and one questions swimming inside of them. Shock and bewilderment held my mouth open while my jaw hung there in disbelief. Dwayne was all of 21 years old with how many kids? Dwayne Jr., Shayla, Latoya, and Latonya, four freaking kids.

His mama read my mind saying, "That's right, four children, three different mothers and ain't minding none of them." She let out an exasperated sigh while turning towards her son. "Am I telling lies, Dwayne?"

I looked at him to see if he would deny the charges, but he wouldn't look at me. Hands tucked into his jeans pocket for warmth with the frigid air giving him sniffles he just stood there, the object of my dumbfounded stare. I was like, say something fool, but the fool wouldn't even say anything. The pieces were beginning to come together. In addition to the baby riding his mama's hip the little girl hanging onto her dress belonged to Dwayne too, plus twin girls, Latoya and Latonya he abandoned in New York. He'd conveniently forgotten to mention anything about fathering any of them, but now planned on dumping two of his kids off on his momma and ditching them for me. Apparently ditching his kids for dates happened often, but this time his momma had enough.

"Chile, its best you don't waste your time with my son." She said, "he immature and unfocused in life and the boy can't decide whether he want to be a child or a man, so you know what I call him?"

I raised an eyebrow, shrugged my shoulders.

"A man child," she said, "he thought he was a man when he made those babies, but it's not making the babies that makes you a man, it's the responsibility you take for those babies that makes you a man and so far Dwayne ain't take none."

Shayla, the little girl standing to her side, shyly tugged at her grandma's dress to get her attention then squeezed her legs together and squirmed in her pants impatiently to let her know she had to pee. Dwayne's mom placed her hand on the girls shoulder, gave her a slight shrug and in a stern voice instructed her to wait and to hold it. "Grown folks," she scolded, "were talking and were not to be interrupted."

"So basically what you're saying is he doesn't do anything for his kids," I asked watching the little girl dance around holding herself becoming the center of attention and temporarily taking our focus off of Dwayne. If Dwayne wasn't taking care of his children I could believe it. The little girl looked a hot mess. No one cared to wipe her nose. Dried snot settled at her upper lip. No one cared to wash her clothes. A thin, stained, and washed out oversized t-shirt better fitted for a grown man is what somebody decided to dress her in even in 50 degree weather. No one cared to run a comb through her hair and tie it back with pretty bows and barrettes. The chaos on top of her head consisted of nothing but tangles, split ends, and naps on top of naps. With an endless set of dimples sitting on top of irresistibly pinch-able chubby cheeks she would've been a cute chocolate cupcake of a little girl if somebody cared. In her fight to hold her pee in she caught a glimpse of my gaze and immediately clenched up tighter to her grandma to hide her face from me.

Dwayne watched her too until her face completely disappeared in her grandma's dress and when she no longer held our attention he jumped back into the conversation by letting out a whimper and sucking his teeth, "Man, whatever. I do a lot for my kids."

"Like what?" She wanted to know and so did I. "What exactly is it that you do for them, Dwayne?" She made circles of tender pats on the baby's back and snuggled him closer to her chest creating a nest of warmth and affection. Our raised voices, harsh tones and bitter emotions entangled with the cold raw air made him cry.

"When was the last time you tucked them in bed or read them a book or took them to the park or the zoo? Let me know when the last time you did any thing that amounted to anything for your children."

Not wanting to be challenged, like a grown unattached single man who didn't have to give account of his actions, answer to anyone or make any apologies Dwayne ignored his mother and ran his hand over the dent in his truck once again bruised over the imperfection, sore over the eye sore laying in the middle of the hood and enraged over what rage had done.

"That's sad," I said watching his nonchalant attitude. The baby cried his little lungs out, but Dwayne's priorities gave way to responsibility. Blasé about his kids, his responsibility as a father, his mother's words, everything was of no concern to him, except that stupid truck.

"It's a damn shame is what it is," she said snuggling the baby up tighter to her to protect him from January's rugged wind.

"Yall women don't understand." Dwayne raised his voice an octave to compete over the baby's cry. "If you all tried to look at things from our angle sometimes then you would see that it's not just us. A brother be out here trying, but you females don't give us no kind of motivation to step up."

His momma and I exchanged glances, we both shook our heads and rolled our eyes at him. He went on, "I'm gonna put it to you like this, momma." His breathing was choppy, frustration level metering off the charts. "Taneika rushed DJ to the emergency room 'cause his skin was burning up, had to get all kinds of medications and antibiotics to treat what turned out to be an ear infection and to bring his fever down and how did I find out? Two weeks after the fact when I got the bill forwarded to my address. I barely even see my son, but now I'm 'posed to pay the gotdamn hospital bill."

The baby's' cry heightened and in return so did Dwayne's. Daddy and son both on pins and needles riding the same sound wave trying to push each other off. My ears writhed in pain over the audio pandemonium. "Ain't you make the baby, who else supposed to pay?" His momma fired back adding to the commotion. Anger caused her Caribbean accent to grow thicker, but the thicker her accent grew the harder it was to understand her words.

"What about Christmas, huh?" Dwayne's eyes locked with mine, but I just sucked my teeth and looked away so he could direct his attention on over to his momma. "Shayla's mama took her to take Christmas pictures at the mall and I don't even have one in my wallet to show my friends because I have yet to see them my damn self. See."

Out of his back pocket came a brown snakeskin wallet with his initials D.R. embroidered on the front flap. Inside were old receipts and the plastic slots held debit cards, a Texas driver's license, a gym pass and wallet sized pictures of a few unidentified females, some in sexy poses. All of it scattered across the concrete in his attempt to prove he wasn't solely at fault.

"She talking about if I wanted a picture of my daughter I should've took her to the mall and paid for it myself. But since I ain't pay, I can't have none. Then the twins' moms, all the drama she done caused in my life. A nigga can only take so much, nah mean? That's why I stay away from 'em and that's why I don't bother to call they asses."

"Oh okay, yeah right, *that's* why," I sneered.

"My baby's mothers, even though we don't get along, we 'posed to squash all that when it come to our kids, pretend like we like each other or at least be cordial for they sake, but these money hungry hoes too busy bumming to see it like that."

Dwayne rested both of his hands on his hips, he blew an aggravated breath and shook his head as if he was just now acknowledging the depth and the degree of his own stories. As if his irresponsible sexual history was playing out as a miniseries in his mind, *Life and Times of the Evil baby mama's* and he'd now gotten a chance to press the button and watch. He was telling tales of not one, not two, but of his three baby momma's and their secret conspiracy to exclude him from his children's lives while taking all of his money in the process. How he became entangled in the twisted saga was a series of bad choices and careless mistakes combined with stupidity, but in his mind he was the victim while they were the villains.

"It's like I don't even exist so you know what?" he said and this time he banged his fist into where his mom had banged it earlier, adding a deeper, more pronounced injury to the truck, "I don't. I don't help with nothing 'cause my baby's moms, the courts, the whole damn system treat me like I ain't nothing. Nothing but a child support check."

"Listen to me," His mother roared out yelling all of the chaos. As crazy looking as she was in that big tent sized dress and house shoes she still demanded and commanded all of our respect. When she spoke our lips stayed sealed. Even the baby had calmed down and somehow was now at peace with the world sucking on his own fingers.

"Your father left me *and* he left you, Dwayne," She said, piercing stare escorting her no nonsense tone. "I was young with no education, new to this country and poor with a little child to take care of, but I did the best I could do with what little I had."

She got in his face, cornered him against the truck making sure he couldn't ease away. "Do you know how many times I wanted to walk away, how many times I nearly threw my hands up and said to hell with this? Many times, but you are my child. My flesh and blood, do you understand what that means?" She gritted her teeth and sighed.

"No matter if I was sick, no matter how tired I was and no matter how mad at the world I was over my situation I still had an obligation to you. It was my duty to clothe, feed and do all the extra things I did to make sure you was happy and safe."

Her tone softened. "So what I'm saying to you is if you can look at these babies and not feel the same responsibility to them that I had to you then I'm sorry I didn't raise a better man."

He stood there again silent, gagged and bound by his mother's undeniable love for him, yet emotionless on how to have those same feelings for his own children. His father slipped out of his life long ago never to look back to see the dusk clear behind him because if he did he would have seen the legacy he left behind consisted of a cycle of chaos and confusion Dwayne was destined to repeat. The apple never falls far from the tree.

"Well," she said impatiently, and backed away giving him some wiggle room.

"Well what?" Dwayne brushed lint balls off of his t-shirt and shook the rest of his clothing out making sure they didn't have any wrinkles and remained just as crisp and pressed as before.

Her eyes grew as big as golf balls and bulged from their sockets in disbelief at how stupid her son was. "Are you going to step up, be a man and take some responsibility for these children?"

His eyes drifted to the top of his head as if he was truly contemplating whether he wanted to be a parent or not. The time it took, the Jeopardy music should have been playing in the background.

"Let me make it clear for you, okay," his mother said sternly, "Instead of taking her out tonight," she pointed at me, "you need to be taking them out." She gently shook the baby again and scrunched her hand through the tangles on the little girls head to give her scalp a scratch. That's when we noticed a yellow stream running down the girls' legs and feet, pouring into the cracks in the concrete and dampening the ground. Nature's call declined the request to be silenced. Her makeshift potty was a puddle of piss and we all stood in the middle of it.

Dwayne's mama cussed beneath her breath, looked like she wanted to whip her grandchild for wetting her clothes, but knew better than to chastise a child for bodily functions, something she couldn't control. Dwayne, more concerned with the bottom of his Nike's than his daughters' potty training threw his hands up in disgust and backed away from the puddle, from us, from the whole situation.

"Momma, just take them in the house," was all he said.

She rolled her eyes, mouthed a few angry words and snatched up the little girls' hand. With the baby riding her hip she marched away furious, each step wide and more of a stomp than a step. Those worn and weathered house shoes click-clacked all the way to apartment 209 in building C. And without so much as twisting her neck to look back at the disappointment she called a son, the whole neighborhood could hear the crash from the door slamming shut behind them.

We rode in silence all the way back to my apartments. Before dropping me off he had the nerve to ask if he could make it up to me by taking me out the following night. I answered by slamming the door of his truck and telling him to lose my number. In my mind Dwayne was out of touch, out of line and outrageous for apparently having a problem with his wages being garnished from his paycheck each week and not having to do any of the hard stuff like spending time with them, changing diapers, bike rides in the park or lunches at McDonalds. He'd left that to his babies' mamas and to his own momma, seeing nothing wrong with being a part-time dad.

What kind of woman would I be to unequally yoke myself with someone as ignorant of his obligations as a father and as a man as Dwayne? What would happen to our child if I got pregnant? Next year would I be standing in line behind his other babies' mamas begging him to spend some quality time with my baby? Or would I just be angry and bitter for being foolish enough to think my baby was more special than the other four and somehow the fifth time around he'd finally decide to step up to the plate instead of just sitting on the side lines like parenting is a spectator sport. Finding myself accidentally on stage of that production between Dwayne and his mom, listening to him recite a script of excuses and half hearted attempts at excuses unfortunately not uncommon of today's men was for me a personal warning not to get caught up in the same mix up many sisters played around in only to find themselves stuck, knee deep in baby daddy boo-boo.

But, first off let me say that not all Black dads are dead beat, not even most Black fathers are dead beat. There are a lot of brothers out here handling their business, raising their children and doing a mighty good job at it. Some have even had the script flipped on them and have been left by their baby's mother to raise the children by themselves. So we do recognize and appreciate the ones who with tired arms and weary feet try to overcompensate for all the other Black men not doing their jobs, the ones who will get stereotyped into the deadbeat dad category simply because their skin is dark, guilty by assumption, guilty by association.

Props also need to be given to those brothers who never knew their own dads, those who possess a silent anger towards the faceless men who they could never call daddy, therefore set out to be better fathers than what they had. Kind of like a competition with the invisible man, "*I can be a better man than you ever were*". There are some out here trying and those are the ones we appreciate and thank. But then there're the ones who aren't and that's who I'm addressing because the impact of their absence is so deep.

Drugs, jail, and unemployment together with a community that is all too accepting of their absence all play a big part in the disappearance of Black fathers, but out of all the reasons Black men come up with for walking away and not doing what they need to be doing concerning their kids is conflicts with the baby's mother. Baby mama drama is the one excuse continually repeated, reused, and reiterated time and time again.

Now why is it that some brothers seem to lose the desire to raise their children because they can't stand their baby's mother? They want to slap her with that played out, *the baby ain't mine* line because they claim she slept with their cousin, best friend, or whoever, but in reality they're just saying *since I don't like you no more the last thing on earth I want is to be connected to you for the rest of my life through this child and if that means I'm out, I'm out.* The child could be a splitting image of him, forehead, eyes, nose and all, but he's going to lie and deny and call her every kind of hoe in the book so he won't have to take responsibility. The paternity test is like 99.999 percent accurate, but since there's that .001 percent possibility then hey, *the baby ain't mine. See you when I see you, peace.*

A brother is gone like he was never even there and his reasoning for it has nothing to do with his own selfishness or immaturity, but instead it's his baby's mother; her drama and her big mouth. Understand the twisted logic of deadbeat dads, though. See, while his baby's mama is used as a scapegoat for his cold isolation and quick desertion of anything that even looks like parental responsibility he'll just as quickly skimp over the fact that just a year or two ago he chose to drop his drawers and have reckless unprotected sex with her. Nobody tricked him, forced him, or oops he accidentally found himself butt naked, slipped on the condom he forgot to put on and fell in between her open legs.

I don't believe there are any instances of conception under these circumstances in recorded history. The pregnancy may not have been planned, but sleeping with her was an option he very willingly chose to make. She was loud and rowdy from the jump, but now since she's had the baby suddenly she's too much, too demanding and crazy.

Why he couldn't figure out she was crazy before the baby came along is the million dollar question. Knowing that any woman he lays down with is a potential mother to his child should have caused his drawers to pause, but dogs in heat don't rationalize they react. Circulation is cut off to the brain, blood is pumping to the nether regions at 110 miles per hour, the condom gets left in his wallet, lust clouds his judgment and boom, nine months later the genetic codes of two strangers or two people who are completely incompatible are forever intertwined.

It is awkward and uncomfortable to raise a child with someone you don't love, don't like or don't really even know for that matter. Values conflict, parenting styles clash and more often than not when the relationship, commitment and the feelings aren't there for the mother it's hard to maintain a relationship, commitment or feelings for the child.

Brothers, the good looking woman agreeing to go home with you after the after party could morph into a psychotic monster over the course of nine short months. Think. Be careful who you lay down with. Don't let just any and anybody have your child. Even if she's a girlfriend marriage vows haven't been exchanged, which speaks volumes to the level of commitment and love you feel towards her. A girlfriend isn't good enough to make a baby with if she's not good enough to marry. And if she *is* good enough to marry, but you're simply not financially or emotionally ready to commit to a marriage how on earth are you ready to commit to the hard work and overwhelming responsibilities of raising babies?

A lot of you all aren't which is why with packed bags and rags out the door you go, too soft to parent through tiny rifts with the mother and way too weak to withstand the arguments, disagreements, and occasional fights that may come as a result of her being just as tired, frustrated and disappointed as you are over the circumstances.

Black women love their children hard and dearly, but are emotionally bankrupt and drained from single parenthood. Some secretly crave the courage to turn their backs on it all and to walk away from the responsibility just as cool and unaffected as some of you, but because a mothers' heart is bound to her womb and anything to inhabit it she stays, most of the time. It is both a joy and a burden women are blessed to possess.

A man's body isn't crafted to support and nourish a growing fetus. A man can't experience the release of certain hormones blended together to create the strong emotions tied to giving birth. A man can't bond with his baby through breast feeding or any of the other little heartwarming biological moments that naturally occur between mother and child. Because of this men sometimes do not naturally adhere to their children. Sometimes they need a push, a boost, some type of motivation to get them up and running into the role of responsible-loving father.

For a man to be in love with the mother of his child, I'm talking about head-over-freaking-heels is one of the best motivators. What man is going to refuse bread to the child of a woman he is swept up in a whirlwind romance with? He will never deny paternity, in fact he will brag to every body on the block how that's *his* beautiful brown baby. Providing for the baby isn't an issue because he's fulfilling a responsibility to the child he produced with the love of his life.

Changing dirty diapers may not be his thing, but he'll be in there wiping up poop like it's his pleasure, buying food and formula with the last ten dollars in his pockets, exchanging the Saturday night club scene for a quiet night rocking the baby to sleep. You see step fathers doing the same thing for their wives' children. It doesn't matter if they aren't his biological children. Because he's in love with her, anything that's a part of her he will love too. For a brother, the first step towards being a better father is working on having a better relationship with the mother.

If more women would play their part and stop giving these men a hard time, making it difficult for them to father their children and using the children against them by saying dumb stuff like, "if he don't want to be with me, he can't see the kids," or "I'm putting him on papers," even though he's been paying his fair share without having the courts involved then I think some of these men would be a little more motivated to step it up. Some of them. Quit with the, "he cheated on me, he did this to me or he did that to me". Cut it out. It doesn't matter what he did to *you*, just because he was a lousy husband, boyfriend, or one night stand doesn't mean he'll automatically be a lousy father. Ease up, give him a chance, stop being so critical and scrutinizing every single thing he does wrong. He'll make some mistakes, every parent does, including you, but so what. Give your baby's father a chance to learn just as you've been given the chance to learn.

Understand that more than likely you have a strong support system; your mom, aunts, sisters, cousins and friends who are there to show you the ropes of single parenting, give you money or advice and baby sit when you need a break. On the other hand your child's father may not. It's unfortunate, but if he is less than a great dad it's probably because nine out of ten times he didn't have his father around and no other men around to show him how it's done.

You may say, "forget him and how hard he has it", the rocky past you've had with him may cause you not to have any sympathy for your child's father, but at least for the sake of your children be a little more understanding, supportive and encouraging. Sisters, for the sake of your children get over yourselves. It's not always about you, boo.

Aside from the rancid relationship with the baby's mom, I'm

betting that a lot of missing dads are also hiding out due to the shame they feel by not having a job, many times meaning not having the money to even buy their child a Happy meal from McDonald's.

The high unemployment rate that this country is facing, which is always highest among Blacks make it even harder for Black men to provide and to contribute. When a man can't provide or contribute financially it eats away at who he is and how he feels about himself as a man. No man, black, white, yellow, red or brown feels good about himself with empty pockets and a dried up bank account, but for a Black man with the chips already stacked against him, i.e. his skin color, those feelings of inadequacy, incompetence and worthlessness are two, three, sometimes four-fold.

As a man he is told he has to be the breadwinner, but he's broke and embarrassed that he can't buy his kid anything or do anything besides make empty promises of what he'll do next month or next year or later on in the year or at the end of the year for Christmas. In some situations when he comes around the mother of his child is looking at him like he's sorry, making snide-insulting remarks to highlight the fact that once again he's lost his job or still hasn't found one or just plain lazy for not looking for one. The child may want sneakers, bikes, Barbie dolls, computers and video games, but because he has to come around empty handed all the time looking like a chump, he simply stops coming around. He's over there thinking, "I'm gonna go see them when I get my stuff straight, when I move into a nicer apartment or when I get a car to take them out." Five years might've gone by since he's last seen his children, but he's still saying, "when I this" and "when I that".

It might be an ego thing and for some brothers their ego is their worst enemy, but a Black man has got to humble himself and get over the way he thinks he's seen through the eyes of his child or the child's mother. Brothers, for the sake of your children get over yourselves. It's not always about you either, boo. Spending time with your kids shouldn't have anything to do with spending money nor should your financial situation determine whether or not you play an active role in your child's life. Being broke is no excuse for being a deadbeat, plain and simple. When it's your weekend, take them for the weekend; don't drop them off at your momma's house for her to feed and entertain them. No car, hop on the bus. Don't live on the bus line, walk it out. Got bad knees or the weather is bad, stay home, keep them at your apartment (no matter how small or un-kept or how many roommates you share it with) to watch a made-for-television movie.

Quality time cost nothing but time, so its time for all excuses to end. There really are no excuses for not taking care of your children, just lies, some more lies and some more lies after that. We know the weight of raising children is heavy, we know it can be time consuming, we know sometimes its nerve wrecking, and of course expensive, but something we also know is that together we can lighten each others load. The key is together. So as many excuses as brothers throw out I'm going to throw it right back.

No one specific thing is to blame for our lack of fathers, just a collection of factors added up through the years shown now in a gapping hole of where we are and where we need to be. Each year the gap seems to grow larger, each day we drift just a little farther away from the promise land, but the encouraging news is that for us the promise land still exists and getting there is not at all hopeless or too big a task to tackle.

Fathers can still reconcile with their families before our children become casualties of the war going on in our communities; before our sons commit a catalogue of crimes and a list of sins without so much as a guilty conscience or before their lack of better teaching forces them to repeat the same mistakes made by their own daddy's. Our precious little girls are waiting by the window in their lacy yellow dresses, eyes soaked with tears waiting for their daddies love to wipe them away, waiting for their daddies to fulfill their promises as fathers and as men.

For all the trifling, good for nothing, lazy so called "men" who will passively nod their heads, roll their eyes and turn a deaf ear to our urgings and who will continue on making babies without taking care of their obligations remember that God is watching and taking notes. *"...If any one does not provide for his relatives, and especially for his own family, he has disowned the faith and is worse than an unbeliever" (1 Timothy 5:8).* It is a grave sin in the eyes of God not to provide for your children. If you're young and don't want to be tied down don't lay down so you won't even be in a situation where you'll have to chose between your freedom, your fun, your money or your children.

Brothers, whatever situation you find yourselves in always do your best to be there for those children. It sounds like a cliché, but those children our truly our future and as the old African proverb states, 'It takes a village to raise a child'. Just remember it is our children who will one day sustain our village.

Jail and the Injustice System

I remember sitting there paralyzed with fear, literally unable to move at work one day. Leroy, a co-worker of mine who I became friends with over the long summer months at my boring part-time job at a call center rolled over to my cubicle in his swivel chair, slyly whispered in my ear with breath tart enough to turn my eye lashes into ashes and told me he was carrying a gun. If anything was said after that I didn't hear it or the telephones ringing, the clicking of computer keys being typed or the chatter of fellow employees swirling around us in the rest of the room. I couldn't hear a thing, but I could read the expression on his face as he rolled back out of my space. It simply said that if somebody pissed him off today there was no telling what might happen. He was under a brick load of stress. The *weight-of-the-world-pressed-down-on-my-shoulders, I'm-about-to-lose-my-mind, don't-push-me-cause-I'm-close-to-the-edge, it's-like-a-jungle-sometimes-it-makes-me wonder-how-I-keep-from-going-under* type of stress.

Imagine a thirty something year old high school dropout, GED recipient with two kids already and a pregnant girlfriend at home working as a telemarketer along side teenagers and college students making just barely above minimum wage plus a tiny percentage in commission. With minimum wage at the time being barely seven dollars an hour, tell me who can seriously live off that? Seven dollars an hour for grown folks in the state of Texas created an environment where too many people just sat at home collecting unemployment, welfare, selling drugs, robbing, stealing anything but make an honest living.

Well this particular co-worker of mines honest living was proving to be non-livable and since a person can only take so much, I guess this was his limit. Aside from that, picture him coming to work the day before only to be told this would be his last couple of weeks on the job. Because of the slumping economy combined with low sales, the company was trimming the fat and had to cut back on payroll. Sixty five employees just got down sized to less than forty. Leroy along with a bunch of other panicked and pissed off soon to be unemployed workers could expect their last paycheck at the end of the month.

"These bastards done picked the wrong nigga." That was the first I heard after unfreezing from my initial shock and floating back into reality. The second thing, "I'm a grown man. I got bills to pay, rent, a baby on the way too. I aught to go down to human resources and light all of 'em up." His words were loaded with so much anger his face turned red and I could see purple and blue veins popping up all over his forehead. Leroy was a light weight, light skinned brother from Port Arthur, a little town in Southeast Texas by the border of Louisiana so every bit of distress showed up on his face as color.

A nervous twitch overtook my body paired together with a feeling of uneasiness just being close to someone who I now labeled as a ticking time bomb. An explosive temper and a hand gun with deadly potential neatly tucked away in the folds of his khaki pants transformed him into Satan's right hand man. Like a pot of boiling broth ready to seep over the edges from intense pressure, he needed to be cooled down. Soothing words of understanding and encouragement, I thought could be the perfect salve.

"You have a lot of reasons not to do anything, you know, stupid, starting first with that unborn baby of yours." This was me, Ms. Level headed throwing out whatever it took to calm him down. I'm not used to Black people going off like this. As a people we have so much going on in our lives that we're usually good at dealing with pressure. From being born into broken homes riddled with poverty, then experiencing racism, prejudice, fighting stereotypes and having to fight just about everything else every step of the way Black people deal with stress and strain just as gracefully as it can be dealt with. This was totally new to me.

Our supervisor Mr. Lambert, a seemly old White man with a Santa Claus beard and pot belly to match popped out of his corner office to make sure everyone was doing what he paid us to do, rather than gossip, goof off and ride the clock, things we often did instead. From time to time during the course of our shift he would stick his head out of the office door, which he always kept open to answer any questions we had or to quiet down the excess conversation so we'd get back to work.

Although furious and ranting, Leroy lowered his voice to maintain a cool whisper along with an even cooler demeanor careful not to attract Mr. Lambert's attention. "You know I been coming to work on time everyday for the last eight months straight." His nostrils flared between paranoid eyes carefully bouncing around the room making sure he wasn't attracting an audience. "Never called in sick. Not one damn day in eight whole months."

I nodded to let him know I sympathized and gave him an "uh-huh" for added affect.

"I'm the hardest working person up in here, reach my quota and then some every month but these mofos gonna let *me* go. Tell me what kind of sense that make?"

"Makes no sense to me," I said then said, "But maybe this is a blessing in disguise," hoping he would use spiritual eyes wide enough to see beyond the moment. Maybe losing this job would open up an opportunity for him to find a better job, I figured.

Thumbs franticly tapped against the desk, an irritated and agitated signal from a man unable to look at the glass as half full, a man who wanted to self destruct and destroy everyone else over the loss of a low paying, low skilled job with no benefits and no upward mobility.

He asked in a hostile pitch, "how in the hell is not being able to pay my rent or take care of my family a blessing?" The corners of his cracked lips white and milky.

The computer screen in front of me flashed signaling that my automated dialer had reached a live contact so I switched on my headphones reading the sales pitch verbatim just as we'd been taught in training class. Under the circumstances I didn't care about making a sale or doing my job, but it was a welcomed distraction buying me time to think of a response.

In the meantime Mr. Lambert made his way over to our area making small talk along the way with some of the other employees. When he got to our station noticing the angst on my face and the troublesome expression on Leroy's he put one of his hands on Leroy's shoulder and rested the other on mines. With Mr. Lambert standing over us the tension that dwelt in our midst could be felt, it was Louisiana gumbo-thick.

He smiled at Leroy, "Tyrone Smith, how's it going?"

"The name's Leroy. Leroy Mitchell, man," Leroy said irritated at the mix up.

"Good ol' Leroy Mitchell. Pardon my mistake, but I just wanted to come by and let you know that I'm sorry my superiors won't let me retain a good employee like yourself. You're a real asset to this company and I hate to see you leave."

"Yeah man, you and me both," Leroy said and placed his own headphones on hinting that he didn't want to be bothered. His shoulders tensed up as he scooted closer to the computer screen in front of him creating a bubble warding others out of his personal space.

Oblivious and unaware Mr. Lambert kept running his mouth, that annoyingly slow deep southern accent amplified the intensity of the conversation. He even firmed the grip his hands held on our shoulders.

"I'm hoping for things to pick up around here shortly so we can get back on track, get on our feet again, but until then we've got to do what's best for business. You understand?"

Hovering over us Mr. Lambert couldn't see Leroy's ugly distorted monster face. He shot up the middle finger and underneath his breath he told Mr. Lambert where he and the rest of the company could go and where they could all shove the business, but Mr. Lambert couldn't see or hear that either. Leroy just nodded his head and grunted.

"It's really nothing personal," Mr. Lambert assured and this time he was directing his spotlight towards me although I hadn't been one of his employees given the pink slip. I nodded my head and grunted too, fake smiled silently wishing Mr. Lambert to just leave us alone, but he didn't. For whatever reason he felt the need to isolate himself from the rest of the company and remove himself from any blame or responsibility for the layoff. Mr. Lambert was a people person, always the nice guy seeking the praise and approval of others, hated playing the bad guy. If someone had a complaint he tried his best to get it resolved and if there was no solution he made sure to let them know he tried his best to come up with one.

"For the record I just want you to know that I did fight hard for you my friend," He said focusing back on Leroy.

With the gun giving him steel courage, Leroy's tongue loosened, "Did you fight for me like you did them pimple faced White boys over there?" He yelled pointing to a group of White teenagers who just like me had been among the lucky ones still holding on to their jobs.

"Pardon?" Mr. Lambert's face turned red with embarrassment or sheer shock at the outburst. A few nosey heads turned to find out what was going on followed by giggles, shoulder shrugs and inquiries from people trying to get the scoop, but Mr. Lambert took control of the situation by making them turn back around to their computers to do their work.

He smoothly maintained his professional demeanor by keeping his composure. "I assure you the deciding factor had nothing at all to do with race. It all boiled down to job performance and numbers. This is a telemarketing firm and those with the highest number of sales are the one's we've chosen to remain with us. And while your sales were impressive, they just weren't as high as some of the others."

"Yeah, whatever," Leroy said dismissing Mr. Lambert and focusing his bloodshot eyes on the screen in front of him.

"It shouldn't be difficult for a hard working young man like yourself to find another gig soon, Tyrone," Mr. Lambert said.

"It's Leroy," Leroy said growing more frustrated by the minute "My name is Leroy, not Tyrone, Man." He was talking to Mr. Lambert, but looking at me with his peripheral vision. Weeks ago Tyrone turned in his letter of resignation, cleared his desk, polished up his resume and shuffled out the door in order to put his Associates degree in business to work. He hadn't slaved for this company since. Tyrone and Leroy, two different men with two different personalities and respectably two different life paths. We're not all alike and we definitely don't all look alike. Why some White people fail to see that confuses me, but as obnoxious as they are I wouldn't automatically label them as racist. Ignorant maybe, but for the most part harmless. That's what I hoped Leroy was thinking as his eyes pierced into mine and not thinking of doing something stupid with that gun in his pants, something that would get him fifteen to twenty years upstate. I gulped not able to tell.

Mr. Lambert went on, "My apologies again, but in fact there's a good chance I might even have a few leads and business contacts for you myself, Lee-roy," Mr. Lambert said exaggerating the name to emphasize the fact that he'd gotten it right this time.

"That is if you change that attitude of yours," he added and patted Leroy on the shoulder like they were old buddies. Leroy, floating between sanity and insanity tip-toed all the way over to the crazy side and snapped. "Man, if you don't take your damn hand off of me there's a good chance you might not have a hand in a minute."

Mr. Lambert quickly snatched his hand away and just as quickly Leroy jumped out of his seat. The cord connecting his head phones to the computer got tangled with the wires hooked up to the old school rotary phone and computer until they, just like Leroy, snapped too. My heart skipped two beats as I flew out of my swivel chair, seeking refuge from the scene sure at that moment Leroy would pull out his gun and start blasting.

All up in Mr. Lamberts' personal space, just like moments ago Mr. Lambert invaded his, Leroy twitched, his body trembled, and his lips quivered like a crack head suffering from withdrawal symptoms, scarred maybe of what he was capable of committing at that moment. Our supervisor, a good man caught in the crossfire of an irate employee trembled too, but the rush of testosterone in his body made him stand firm, wouldn't let him back down from Leroy.

All eyes were now on the commotion between Mr. Lambert and Leroy and it seemed as if time had slowed down or simply stopped. Two grown men in fancy clothing reduced to angry bulls, ready to charge, but waiting for the other to buck. The drop of a pin could've been heard as everyone in the call center waited for the next scene to unfold.

"Young man I'd advise you to have a seat and don't make anymore of a scene than you already have," Mr. Lambert stiffened his posture, cleared his throat and deepened his voice to execute his authority.

"Man, you have a seat," Leroy said pushing Mr. Lambert back into a row of empty chairs so hard he lost his balance and collapsed to the floor taking a few of the chairs down with him. His glasses flung off and got crushed underneath the rubble. A bad toupee came off too leaving the shiny bald spot on his head underneath exposed.

Leroy stood over the wreckage he caused, smiled the smile of someone satisfied with the destruction of his own hands, a smile that held no remorse for causing harm to another human being. Some people rushed to Mr. Lambert's aid, while others reached for their cell phones to call downstairs to security or the police or whoever. "You're gone buddy. Today," Mr. Lambert cried on the ground aching.

Leroy laughed like *so what?* yesterday he'd already been told he was going to be laid off so in his mind he had nothing to lose.

With assistance from some of the employees Mr. Lambert stood to his feet, but couldn't stand all the way straight. The wind had been knocked out of him and he was fat, a good thirty or forty pounds over weight with too much blubber swimming around his waist, arms and legs. "You're gone." He huffed and panted, crouched like he was sitting on an invisible toilet and rubbed his big belly trying to get back his breath, "right now, get your things and get the hell out of here."

"Man, you ain't got to tell me, I'm out, but let me tell you and everybody else up in here something first," Leroy said and hopped up on one of the desk wobbling, nearly breaking his legs and all of his other important limbs on the way up as he slipped on a stack of papers sending them flying. Laughter from our co-workers set the temperature on his temper soaring as he regained his balance.

"Hey y'all in the back shut the fuck up and listen."

His bloodshot eyes took their time piercing into each one of our eyes individually demanding we wipe the smirks off our faces. Something just told us he was serious as a diagnosis of terminal cancer. Although I hadn't laughed up to that point and wasn't going to laugh because I just knew he was at his breaking point, the giggles and chit-chatting from everybody else ceased in fear of what this crazy co-worker would do next. Every second more sweat accumulated on my palms and my armpits were soaked. My nerves had me a nervous wreck and although he hadn't whipped it out, the pistol in his pants still held me hostage.

"This a little announcement for all the Niggas up in the room… my bad I mean Black folk, African Americans whatever the hell they wanna call us now." Leroy shifted about, blinked too many times and continued twitching. "Negroes, listen up. We made this company, naw, naw we made this country and we been getting screwed with no K-Y jelly for years my nigga."

Leroy stumbled and nearly lost his balance again. He gripped a cubicle divider for support while pointing down at us with a finger he couldn't quite keep steady.

"Stay off of heroin boys and girls, it will mess you up. I'm messed up right now so I should know," he said steadying himself, "But I ain't that messed up okay, so here me out." He managed to stop twitching long enough to prove just that.

"I was locked up for six years over some bullshit I ain't even much do. See 'cause I looked like somebody who was doing it, I hung around fools who was doing it and I had the attitude of somebody who was doing it, but I ain't do it, for real. I spent six long ass years in a metal box caged like a animal over something I ain't had shit to do with." More twitching.

"So I gets out and here I go tryna make something of myself, working for these prissy ass White folks for chump change, but I'm making a honest living so it's all good. I'm calling peoples house interrupting they dinner to tell them about some damn satellite dish that cost a fucking arm and a fucking leg, but ain't worth shit cause every time it rain they T.V. ain't gonna get no reception. But hey, I gots to lie to them and tell them how wonderful it is, beg them for they fucking money just so I can reach my damn quota for the month."

Leroy made his lips protrude out as they trembled through the rest of his speech. "Man, these White people don't give a shit about no nigga like me 'cause if they did I'd still have a fucking job. I tried to do things the right way and look what it got me, a one way ticket to the unemployment office. Now I gots to go rob they ass before I end up living in a card board box." Twitching followed by more twitching.

"Now if y'all niggas don't wanna end up eating out a dumpster y'all better listen up." He softened his voice to a whisper and stooped down as if he was letting us in on a big secret. "We can fight this y'all. Yep, we can file one of them suits against them for discrimination or wrongful termination or some shit like that. Take they ass to the cleaners and hang them out to dry just like they been doing us all these years. Is y'all with me?"

You could hear some people holding back laughter, others shocked by his outlandish behavior and wild outburst just stared at him in disbelief, while most of the Black people hung their heads in shame, embarrassed for the crazy fool up on the desk making our race look bad. Leroy gazed down into the congregation of co-workers looking for someone to back him up, and when he got no support he stammered around and mumbled something angry under his breath like, "Fuck y'all" in callous tones. In his mind he was a modern day Farrakhan up on an improvised podium feeding a lost flock his extremist views of revolution and rebellion against the Man and his unjust system. To us he'd gone bananas, as fanatical as those people who run from the cops thinking they'll get away even with helicopters, news cameras and state troopers trailing them. This is how Leroy was, as thrilling to watch as a high speed police chase because of its potential to end in violence.

Mr. Lambert was off in a corner straightening his toupee back on his head trying to make it blend in with his side burns. Leroy squinted bringing Mr. Lambert back into focus, watched him smooth out his hairpiece in a frenzy, then watched him scoop up pieces of his broken glasses from the carpet. Leroy's bloodshot eyes bulged from their sockets and stayed on Mr. Lambert as if he'd just now come to a shocking realization of what he'd done. Like he'd instantly sobered up from a drug induced high and was now suffering from a serious hang over served with a side dose of regret.

"Aw man, I fucked up," he said and jumped off the table, again nearly severing his limbs. Panicky and breaking into a cold sweat my friend exemplified the melt down of a Black man whose soul hadn't been nurtured in childhood, whose sensibility had been substituted for insanity and whose social values had been shaped by a collection of stereotypical images on T.V., the local hip-hop radio station and the poor neighborhood he'd grown up in with it's distorted views of manhood and morals.

Leroy's foundation was unstable and weak and quickly disintegrating under pressure right before our eyes. He was an ex-convict high on a little powdery white drug called heroin, the only thing he could see to numb his mind from the tirade of being tossed around in a system set up for only a few to succeed and many more to fail, the American injustice system.

To everyone's relief Leroy stumbled on over to the exit knocking a few stray boxes over and kicking them out of his way as he left. Before completely vanishing behind the doors into the hallways where the muscle head security guards were sure to be hot on his trail he summed up the confusion and the desperation of a million Black male victims of the injustice system by extending his trembling hands up to the sky and asking, "what a nigga 'sposed to do now?"

For some people this is all they know and sadly all they'll ever allow themselves to know; pain, suffering, confusion, anger and the reaction to these emotions, revenge, which will ultimately lead to more pain, suffering, confusion and anger. It's a cycle that few in his position are enlightened enough or lucky enough to escape. Leroy was one man telling his story through a cracked voice and eyes that showcased a broken spirit, but his reality represented a million others.

That situation could've been fatal, a potentially dangerous criminal could've harmed a lot of people, but the "dangerous criminal" was somebody's brother, father and son and an important part of the Black community. Since he didn't whip out his pistol and go postal he probably never intended to do anything with it to begin with. Digging a little deeper and considering the fact that he would run his mouth and blab to me about a weapon that was never drawn all just seemed like a cry for help.

Unfortunately the cry for help from a lot of Black men isn't a cry, but instead a ferocious scream of anger and rebellion. Leroy's case, while extreme was in no way isolated. Was it an overly dramatic reaction to the common everyday madness that occurs in a Black mans life? Of course it was tremendously radical, but the burden of having to be the breadwinner and constantly falling short, the denial of racism just because now we finally have a Black president and the constant stress without a positive outlet can transform a man into a monster.

Be a man usually means be a monster. It means to act hard, suppress your feelings and pretend like everything is cool when its not. Men are expected to be macho, strong and tough. Outside their expression is stone cold even when their insides are a marshmallowy mush, a soft composition of fear, insecurity, and vulnerability. In a man's mind this façade is what keeps the world intact, but in actuality it's what's ripping the world to shreds and tearing our communities apart.

The suppression of an emotion is a dangerous act because what we think of as suppression is really just ignoring the feeling until it shows up in an ugly new form. Trust and believe it will show up, sometimes sooner than later, sometimes later than sooner, but when it does show up stand back. Black men disproportionately suffer from heart disease, depression, painful ulcers, high blood pressure, and they keel over from heart attacks by the hundreds everyday often times because they suppress their emotions instead of reaching out for help and talking about whatever's bothering them. It's that old pride thing.

Many brothers are too proud to admit that they can't do it on their own, that they're in need of help, that they're tired, that they're lonely, that they're stressed, that they're frustrated, that their feelings are hurt, that they're failing, or even when they're coughing and sneezing, bruised and bleeding, suffering with chest pains and shortness of breath, they're afraid to admit that they're sick and its killing them, literally and emotionally.

Even the first law of thermodynamics, which states *energy is neither created or destroyed, but simply transformed or transferred,* testifies to this fact. Leave an emotionally battered man without council or an outlet to vent his anger, frustrations, or his pain and those emotions won't go away, they will simply transform into stress, which will build, and build and build until BOOM, an emotional breakdown. There you have the Leroy's of the world. There is the making of the drug addicts and the alcoholics and the murderers and the gang bangers and the child molesters and the rapist and the punk domestic violence men who would rather pound their fist into their woman's face instead of deal with the underlying issues that's causing their anger, their frustration, their pain or their need for control. Worst yet, a growing number of brothers find solace in suicide, blowing their brains out underneath the mounting pressures of life and living.

Trace back to their beginnings and you'll see that as destructive as these men are now, they started off as innocent young boys who somewhere along the way became confused about manhood. Confused about their role in society, confused about how to deal with tension, confused about their own emotions and how to display them. For a lot of them there was no strong male example in the home to show them that '*hey, this is okay to do and say or not do and say under these situations and circumstances, this is how you love, respect, and treat a woman, this is how you take care of your responsibilities, this is how you release this negative energy so it won't build up, this is how you succeed in life; hard work, no shortcuts, no free rides, its going to be hard, this is what you'll face, but this is the payoff. This is what it is to be a real man*'.

The conclusion they came to on their own or from the streets or from their homeboys who didn't have good fathers themselves was that in order to exemplify the true meaning of manhood, weakness and any sign of it was to be hidden, neatly tucked away or simply non existent. Like many other words, ideas and concepts, the streets hold its' own meanings for manhood and weakness. Among young Black men weakness could mean crying your eyes out instead of being what they call a man and just sucking it up or getting your point across in as few words as possible. Running off at the mouth is for females, men shut up and handle business.

It doesn't matter that science has proven that crying releases chemicals built up in the body due to stress and that a good boo-hoo releases all of that. It doesn't matter that most women can attest to the fact that having a deep heart to heart convo with someone you trust about a difficulty you're having somehow makes you feel better and better equipped to handle that difficulty. These things don't matter because however hurt a young man may feel, he fears displaying even the slightest sign of vulnerability will have swift and brutal consequences amongst his peers.

Weakness is asking for help instead of figuring it out yourself. Real men don't ask questions, they're just supposed to know and do without directions or instructions. You're the boss, shoot first, ask questions last. Giving directions and orders are for leaders, asking for directions means you're a follower. This same rule of manhood is why so many of our young brothers have serious problems with figures of authority. In their minds, *can't nobody* tell them what to do.

In the streets weakness is seen as loving something too hard or too deeply. For a young man weakness is being loyal to anything other than his mama, his boys, his block or his pursuit of money. Being dedicated to non-sports related school activities or programs to better himself, investing in his education or even becoming infatuated over just one girl as opposed to juggling three or four, gets a brother labeled as soft on some streets. In the poorest projects and ghettos across America where social and physical survival means strength, respect and power, weakness can cost a brother his life.

Somewhere along the course of history the image of a strong Black man became grossly distorted. Too many of our little Black boys are looking at manhood through a fun house mirror, a tainted glass of misconstrued figures. They try to mimic an imaginary image; a gansta, a thug, a pimp, a hustler making fast money with females fighting each other for the front seat passenger side of his expensive ride. They don't see *strong men* waking up at the crack of dawn to catch the bus to work, or to fill out job applications or to beg White people for their crummy minimum wage jobs. To a lot of them *real men* are out hustling, pimping, calling shots, making paper, riding on twenty two inches of chrome, stepping on the gas pedal with expensive kicks, no kind of sweat to even get it.

This idolized life is glamorous, but it's fake. It promotes laziness, discontentment and encourages young men not to think about the future or consequences or to see beyond the moment, but to crave instant gratification instead of the hard work, time and dedication it takes to transform a vision into reality. If this weren't true more Black men would be enrolled in college than wasting away behind bars.

As mentioned before, the old African proverb states, *it takes a village to raise a child* meaning besides parents, teachers, church leaders, neighbors, the extended family and society as a whole all play a role in shaping the values of that child. Just because a child doesn't have a strong family foundation doesn't mean the child should be left to his own devices, left to fend for himself and left to his ultimate demise. Where parents go wrong, because they do time and time again the rest of us should be more than willing to pick up their slack.

For those who think it's not their kids so it's not their responsibility or their problem, wake up and watch the five o'clock news, the six o'clock news, the ten o'clock new. These are America's children and now America's nightmare because they were no ones responsibility. No one cared, took the time, paid attention or invested in their emotional well being. As quickly as you can turn your back on the situation thinking it doesn't affect you, a knife is to your throat or a gun is to your head and now it's affecting you. Now it's your problem.

We all hold a stake in their future and should be making investments into the lives of young Black boys. Whether it's donating time or money to a youth organization, volunteering at a big brother program, taking a neighborhood kid who has no father to a basketball game or inviting one of the neighborhood children over to your house once a week to eat dinner with your family and your own kids, it makes a difference. One day they'll either be dating our daughters or raping our daughters. Today we can open our doors welcoming them into our homes or tomorrow they'll be breaking in through the back door to burglarize us. With or without our knowledge we all contribute to the upbringing of Black boys, so where are *we* going wrong and why are we producing more gang bangers than go getters, more dope dealers than do-gooders, more wards of the state than heads of state?

For one thing, I believe all of our supposedly good institutions that are set up to reinforce the values set by our families or to pick up the slack by establishing values for those who don't have stable families are instead adding to the problem. The public school system, for example is raising a lot of our boys to be future inmates. School therapists and psychiatrist and greedy pharmaceutical companies suggest doping these kids up with all kinds of weird medications for behavioral problems that sometimes don't even exist just so they can sit still for five seconds. Some of our potential future lawyers and doctors, police officers and politicians, engineers and scientist are being poisoned by dangerous drugs that studies published in medical journals have proven to sometimes have unsafe side effects, yet they are approved by the Food and Drug Administration (FDA).

Some of our potential future accountants, entrepreneurs, and college professors are being dumped in the "Special Education" classes written off as Retarded or Learning Disabled or Emotionally Disturbed simply because the parents and the public education system haven't bothered to seek alternative solutions other than medicine or Special Ed to deal with why these kids can't keep still, pay attention or grasp onto the lessons.

In addition, the education systems crazy obsession with testing, assessments, data tracking, data analysis, and data driven instruction has taken the fun out of learning, the learning out of learning and the motivation for Black boys to excel academically. In many urban schools, Black boys are not being taught how to think through a process, be creative or use their natural inclination for hands-on exploration, building, construction and deconstruction, or anything culturally significant to African Americans, but are being forced to choose the best answer on a multiple choice. When funds that schools receive are tied to high performance on tests, programs that make for well-rounded students such as music programs and art programs are halted in replace of test prep materials and after school tutorials.

By the time a child reaches the fifth grade he should be able to read and write a decent sentence, multiply and divide two digit numbers, explain and carry out the steps of the scientific method and at least know the name of past U.S. presidents and their role in history, but a lot of children can't, but are still getting passed along to the next grade and to the next and so forth. Even though a student hasn't mastered certain content and may need to be retained in their current grade for another school year, teachers are reluctant to hold students back because in the eyes of administration it's a poor reflection on their teaching. Even when students are recommended for retention some who have been lazy and did nothing all school year, can simply attend summer school, fake it for about a month and viola, they're passed to the next grade.

By the time a child graduates from high school, that's if he graduates from high school, he is like a fish out of water, choking and disoriented because he can barely compete in the highly competitive job market or the cut throat world of college where teachers won't just pass him along. So what is a young Black man to do after high school or after he's dropped out of high school and is unprepared for the real world? And what is a young Black man to do if he's not qualified for anything besides bagging groceries, taking orders at the drive thru window, working at the car wash or any other low skilled job? Will he bypass minimum wage work and expensive higher education for the quick cash of slanging dope or knocking off corner stores? If poor parenting, poverty, improper public school education and the lure of quick cash are the ingredients then the perfect recipe for a future felon will be brewing.

Inevitably as fate would have it after playing Russian roulette with the law these young men will eventually end up locked up and bent over the knee of the legal system to experience the chastisement of the American injustice system. The same system that has been targeting minorities for years with its ravenous arrangement of unjust laws, corrupt politics, and deceptive legalities. Equipped with sharpened fangs ready to chew a young Black boy to bits behinds its prison walls, then spit him back out into the world as a man, swallowing up his future in the process.

Our system, as most minorities and lower income folks know is riddled with bullets, full of confusing legal loop holes they make brothers jump through only to entangle and trap them. A nineteen year old sitting in the hot seat with two or three slick tongued detectives breathing down his neck might be tricked into making a false confession and sent to prison for a crime he did not commit. What does he know about the Fifth Amendment to the Constitution protecting himself against self incrimination? What does he know about his right to have a lawyer present? Because he is most likely uneducated about the law and his rights as an American citizen and because he is unable to afford decent legal representation his case is haphazardly handled.

The public defender or court-appointed attorney might be some clown fresh out of law school with virtually no experience, no references and no reputation of success in such cases, but is only there to get his measly few dollars from the state and some cases under his belt. In a few rare incidences a bold brother might even gamble with his freedom and try to represent himself. Brought before a Judge who's spent an unreasonable amount of time on campaign fundraising with many of the donors being Prosecutors and District Attorneys, the brother stands a zero to none chance of ever seeing the light of day. With a pound of the gavel he's convicted, sent away and like the old Akon song says, "Locked up".

America stands accused, guilty of incarcerating a record number of Black males behind its filthy, cold, concrete prison walls. Charts or no charts, documented or undocumented, with statistics or without statistics the evidence is laid bare across the jails and prisons in this country. Sociologist, researchers and other social scientists have conducted numerous investigations only to conclude what we've known all along. When most of us can name a friend, an uncle, a cousin or other family member who's in jail, out on parole, on probation, with an existing warrant for their arrest or have a criminal record, then unarguably Black men hold a monopoly on the tail end of the criminal injustice system.

The whys and the how's are an endless list of social sicknesses with virtually no solid root or specific target. If Poverty is to blame for the swelling numbers of Black men in jail, then unemployment is to blame for poverty. If it's the unemployment rate among Blacks, then the lack of formal education is the reason we're unemployed. If Black men aren't educated, then maybe it's poverty that's holding them back. We can't even skimp over the fact that maybe our young ones are out of control and getting caught up in illegal activities because there are no fathers to discipline them in the home because a lot of the fathers are rotting away behind bars themselves.

The blame is wide enough to hide behind all of these factors and until they're really dealt with, not just talked about, preached about, written about and complained about, until then more tax dollars are going to be snatched out of the hands of hard working law abiding citizens to build more prisons when the money would be wiser spent on solid prison prevention plans. Prevention plans like funding to improve public schools, after school programs for young boys and girls, college scholarships, and drug rehabilitation and counseling for addicts and dealers in replace of jail time, just to name a few.

How about some cold hard cash to fund programs that reduce recidivism rates because right now jail is synonymous with revolving door. When a brother has no options or at least none that he finds attractive he'll go back to doing what he knows best, repeating the same old nonsense that landed him behind bars in the first place. Why, because the opportunities for ex-cons to start a new life are scarce.

Look at his job prospects. A regular average Joe with a clean record and a college degree may find himself jobless for months before finding steady decent work, so what can an ex-con with a criminal record expect? How many businesses, companies, and corporations are enthusiastic about hiring a convicted felon? And what if he wants to go back to school to better himself, to get a half decent chance at a half decent job? With financial aid, loans and grants often times limited or denied to people with drug convictions on their records, going back to school is a dream deferred for many ex-cons.

What about finding decent housing? Living arrangements for the newly released can be limited and often times undesirable. Most leasing agents have strict rules against renting apartments to ex-felons and on top of that most ex-cons have bad credit and their dough is low meaning buying a house is out of the question. So where is Mr. Newly-released-from-the-big-house going to lay his head down at night? On somebody's couch, in his momma's basement, in a shelter?

What about the community he's released back into? While he was in jail did he gain the resources he needs to add to the community as a responsible man and a leader, or will he simply be a burden to society, begging and mooching unable to contribute? What about the broken family who has struggled in his absence? Kids? Providing for them? How is he to take care of his children when it's an uphill battle just for him to find a decent job and take care of himself? Without a respectable job and unable to find or afford his own place his role as father and provider is defunct.

What about his woman? How is a man locked up with other stinky hairy legged men supposed to relate to his woman when he's let out? For years his meals and clothing have been provided for, he's been trained when to wake up, told what time he has to go to bed, on a daily basis instructed what to do and how to do it. How is he to get along with a Black woman who's not into babysitting her man or telling him what to do, when to do it and how to do it, but needs a man who is self motivated and takes the initiative, a character trait suppressed by prison? How is the relationship to survive if on the flip side he's on a power trip, finally in a position where he can be in control and now wants to overcompensate for the lack of control he had in prison? Bossing his woman around, making orders and demands, ruling with a rod of iron just because he can, just because he, not the prison guards are now in control.

What about sex and his questionable sexual status? Is he a homosexual now? Did he slip and drop the soap in the showers? Did anyone force anything into his booty or vice versa? Did he like it? Was it consensual? Was it rape? If so was he exposed to the vast array of STD's crawling the penitentiary walls like hepatitis C or HIV? Strong healthy men are being thrown into jail only to come out coughing and itching over what another man gave them when the guards weren't looking (or supposedly not looking). What about that? What about the high number of transmissions among inmates and the women they'll infect when they're released back into the community?

What about the lasting psychological affects caused by what inmates see and experience in prison? What does being locked up all those years with brutal, raw, cold criminals do to his manhood and state of mind, his sexuality and his sanity, his emotional well being? The violence, the abuse from other prisoners, the corrupt prison politics among prison officials, the often times inhumane treatment has got to have some long term effect on a man. Imagine the trauma experienced relatively small time drug dealers when they're cattle rafted into jail with murderers, rapist, pedophiles and psychotics, rubbing elbows with the absolute worst offenders of the law. Instead of re-entering society rehabilitated a lot of times they'll come out more hardened than when they went in. Hardened over what they witnessed in the lock up and by the challenges they now have to face adjusting to life on the outside.

How can a man take pride in himself and become a productive member of society if, after paying his debt to society, society still wants to crucify him, if every corner he turns he's met with a slammed door and a snap judgment? How can he smoothly integrate back into the community and be productive? How can the community do its part by providing some empathy and understanding, compassion and forgiveness? All these questions and many more need answers or at least better answers than what the penal system offers now.

But as of right now the "powers that be" don't seem too pressed to change their unjust system or their rules. Barriers positioned by state agencies and government authorities in the last few years have set into motion certain policies that have reduced or cut funding altogether for community service providers and social services that help keep young men and young women *out of jail*. A lot of states are panicking as they struggle to afford to provide adequate social services as a budget crisis looms over their heads, panicking as they're forced to trim spending and scrimp and save wherever possible.

Funding for public assistance; food stamps, welfare, Medicaid and public housing have all been cut. Funding for education; building new schools, sports and music programs, and after school programs have all been cut. And while tuition at public universities and colleges have increased at some schools by up to 30%, federal grants for college tuition have decreased. Yet every year on average $31,000 in tax payer money is spent to house just one young man or young woman in prison each year.

The government is penny pinching and financially stressed and poor Black men aren't exactly on its list of priorities right now, so rather than trying to dig through America's legal disarray after one of our sons finds themselves buried in trouble we'd do ourselves a favor by focusing on our own methods of prevention. Preventing a young Black man from ever entering the system is the greatest gift we can give to him and to society because once he's there in the "system" trying to get out is like swimming upstream with 100 pound weights strapped to his ankles, he'll eventually sink to the bottom.

Instead of waiting on the system to straighten out the best thing we can do is educate and empower our men and boys in order to put them in a position where they fully understand the ins and outs of the law and ways to smoothly maneuver through it without getting stuck in the kinks. The mentality that they are helpless victims at the mercy of White America's injustice is the real injustice. The mindset that the White man is holding the Black man back is crippling to our young men who are in fact too strong to be held back by anyone and too smart not to know that their actions, their future and their fate is no ones responsibility or fault, but their own.

The system some times is unjust, we see the camera phone videos capturing the police beating our men upside their heads only to get a slap on the wrist, suspension with pay or desk duty because, 'hey' they deserved it for "resisting arrest". We see it every day with stiff mandatory sentences for non-violent offenses that aren't fit for the crime. Crack and cocaine are both dangerous drugs, but get caught with crack, a street drug used primarily by poor Blacks and the penalty is harsher than if you get caught snorting Cocaine, a drug mostly used by upper class Whites. Even with the Fair Sentencing Act of 2010, which overhauled the Anti-Drug Abuse Act of 1986, sentencing disparities still exist.

Our eyes are wide open to these injustices, but can we turn a blind eye to what's really unjust and that's not taking responsibility for our own actions by conveniently pouring all of the blame for our men's high incarceration rates on outside factors. The real injustice is the one we've cast on ourselves for failing to have our men take a deep look in the mirror while we stand behind them gazing into it ourselves, and asking some deep questions. Questions like, who are we as a people? What are we willing to stand for? What are we willing to die for? And what do we refuse to let kill us, physically, spiritually, and emotionally?

Who we are now? Is who we are an accurate representation of what we've come from or have we somehow fallen from grace? Are we really going to blame the White man or the government or the "system" for all the ills going on in our communities or are we going to wake up and realize that in every generation before us from slavery to fighting for our civil rights, change has first started with us. If our schools are run down and our children's teachers are unqualified we have to hold them accountable; show up at school board meetings, petition, write letters, hold fire under the administrators' feet until somebody moves.

If our neighborhoods are dirty, we have to paint over the graffiti, put on the rubber gloves, work a mop, broom, dustpan, Windex, Ajax all of that and clean our neighborhoods up ourselves. If the police are crooked and won't protect us, we have to organize a neighborhood watch and respectively police and protect ourselves. If there is a crack house next door attracting crime, we have to tear it down, brick by brick with our own hands because change is in our own hands. If decent paying jobs are scarce and the few available aren't being given to us, we need to do like the Mexicans, Asians and African immigrants and create our own jobs and keep the wealth those jobs create in our own communities by supporting other Black owned businesses.

How is it that we've so carelessly allowed our children to go uneducated, to go unloved, to run the streets and run wild until they crash and burn, running themselves head on into a brick wall? Why is it that we haven't called our absentee fathers out? We have? Well it's not loud enough. If we were shouting before, we need to be screaming now. Screaming for them to get their butts up and to get their acts together. Screaming for them to come back because they left our mothers and left our children in poverty to fend for themselves, to grow up violent, angry, and mad at the world because daddy didn't give a damn and now neither do the children. Now they act like hooligans, they don't know how to behave in public, have no social training because nobody taught them, momma was too busy at work, working two, sometimes three jobs just to keep the lights on.

Momma didn't have time to watch who her children hung out with or monitor where they went during the day or question whose house her daughter was spending the night at or how her teenage son was able to afford those expensive sneakers even though he didn't have a job. She didn't have time to make it to parent-teacher meetings, show her support at school talent shows, basketball games, or track meets, let alone have time to help them with homework. So with daddy gone and mama at work all day why do we wonder how a young man ends up bags packed on a one way trip to prison?

Why aren't we calling out some of our women when they're so quick to open up their pretty brown unwed legs to make babies they know they can't afford or with men they know aren't any good? Why aren't we telling our young women to think more consciously about the decisions they make, swallow a birth control pill, demand that he wear a condom, or better yet, keep it closed altogether? Why don't we quit being afraid to offend some of the single mothers who so arrogantly think they can raise a generation of Black boys up to be men all by themselves because they think they're superwomen. Why won't somebody jump out of the box and yell to this wave of 'independent' women that the jig is up, it doesn't work, the number of our Black boys who are locked up more often than they are accepted into college screams to the fact that they need their fathers.

After all, next to God, the best prison prevention plan is family. When the family unit is tied together tight, momma has her head on straight and daddy is at home providing both physical and spiritual food, the injustices that will surely come will wilt in comparison to the strength of the family and the protective blessings of God over the family. Can anybody say Civil Rights Movement? We had God, we had the church and we had family, and that's all we needed to get through the lynching's, the cross burnings, and the discriminatory Jim Crow laws. To get through these times we're going to need God, the church, and the family, but right now part of the puzzle is missing. Our families are broken, and we'll never be whole until we piece them back together.

Instead of scratching our foreheads, wondering why America's laws don't work in our favor we might want to look in the mirror and acknowledge the part we play in the decaying souls of our young men. These are our men in jail, these are our children's fathers', these are our sons and brothers and daddy's and uncles and cousins and boyfriends and husbands boo-booing all over their future, flushing it right down the toilet. They belong to us and they are no one else's responsibility, but our own. Wiping the mirror clean and standing in front of our naked reflection places us in a position to see us for who we really are with our beautiful, but broken selves. Then and only then can we control our destiny and change our fate.

Inmates, have a plan before you leave jail or prison, map out a blueprint in your mind and devise an exit strategy on what you're going to do when you get out, how you're going to improve yourself, and what steps you need to take to do so. Join a program while you're in like substance abuse treatment or rehabilitation, vocational job training, Prison Entrepreneurship programs and academic programs if they offer it at your facility. When you're out don't be lazy, actively look for people who can help you get your life together. Don't get discouraged when you've earned your freedom and you're out, yet everybody makes you feel like you're still in by slamming the door in your face just because you have a record. It will happen, you will get turned down from more than a few jobs, it will be hard finding your own place to live, and a lot of women will turn their noses up because they don't want to deal with a man with a shady past, but at all cost don't get so fed up that you end up doing some silly mess that will send you flying back to the jailhouse like a jailbird.

Women, adopt your returning inmate and encourage his efforts to find a job and a better life. Don't blame, criticize, or discourage him by bringing up the past. He's done his time for committing the crime and now it's time for healing, time for moving on to better things and time to let the past be just that, the past. Be smart and cautious, welcoming only those men who passionately want to change their lives back into your lives and back into your homes. Provide compassion, support and high expectations for your sons, brothers, husbands, boyfriends and your children's father when they return.

Black people, if you don't have a loved one in jail, support families that do. A Prison sentence isn't just punishment for the criminal, the family is being punished too. It's hard on the family, sometimes financially, sometimes emotionally, sometimes both, but hard nonetheless. Register to vote and vote for candidates who care about and support humane re-entry policies that establish special services for people coming out of jail; employment recruiting services, services that enable men and their children to emotionally reconnect after incarceration, counseling services for husbands and wives to rebuild their severed marriages, or, anything that makes it smoother for ex offenders to integrate back into society.

Brothers, education is your weapon against injustice so you've got to get it and use it. Now education spans farther than an expensive college course and it reaches way beyond the classroom or a text book. Education is composed of your wisdom to seek God and cultivate a personal relationship with the being who gently orchestrated all the events in history to match up perfectly with his divine will. God is the master of knowledge, wisdom and understanding and education begins first with the acknowledgement of God.

Education is in the whole world around you. Education is in your experiences. It's traveling, learning new cultures, languages and ways of life. It is in understanding the politics of the systems others live in compared to the politics of the system you live in and are affected by. Education is knowing that being a Black man in Brooklyn isn't at all that different from being a Black man in born in Brazil, or the Caribbean, or South Africa, or in the U.K. The language may change, the cultural setting may shift, but wherever you roam or reside on this earth Black man your power is understood, your power is envied, and ultimately your power is challenged.

So challenge them with your education. Always second guess, read the fine print, read between the lines, and don't be fooled into believing anything without first exploring it for your selves. Know your rights, learn about the way the government is run, understand their rules and laws because sooner or later you might be caught up in a situation where that knowledge means life and freedom and the lack thereof means imprisonment or death...mental, spiritual, or physical.

Dippin' n' Mixin':
Dating Interracially

She was lingering in the aftermath of their love making, naked, tangled in the sweat drenched sheets and smoking the herb out of what had to be a courage enhancing stash of grass. Not content with being at the center of the universe or bored with her pampered place up on the world's petal stool she sought to discover the truth behind the rumor of the well endowed Black man.

He was lingering too, maybe a little too long because he had slipped up and forgotten to come home or perhaps just didn't care anymore to cover his tracks. Either way he was blissfully asleep, satisfied, and celebrating the conquest of another woman with snores loud enough for me to hear through the other end of the phone.

Seconds after I dialed my husband's number Snow White picked up as if she paid the cell phone bill, as if she had signed a two year contract with Sprint and although service was terrible was stuck with those high monthly payments, tax, roaming and overage charges as well. More than happy to dish out the dirty details and almost too eager to explain, when I asked who she was and why she was answering my husband's phone, with taunting words she recounted a scene of what'd just went down between the two of them.

Nine o'clock at night after receiving a strange phone call, he slipped out of the house telling me he had to help some co-worker/friend/buddy of his who was stranded on the side of the road after their car broke down as if that co-worker/friend/buddy didn't have free emergency roadside assistance. The thing I didn't know at the time was that this co-worker/friend/buddy of his happened to be the new blue-eyed blonde administrative assistant at his job and after giving her car a jump, instead of coming straight home, he took a detour and went home with her so that she could thank him by giving him a jump. Three hours, two cheap bottles of Boone's Farm watermelon wine and one dime bag of weed later she simply explained that she was done thanking him and would send him home whenever he woke up.

Earlier on I had my suspicions. Would corner him with a full fledged interrogation whenever he came home from "work" smelling like perfume, the inside of a smoky bar, or some other strange scent I could never quite make out. When the click from the bolt unlocking sang its song and he slid his feet through the door, tousled dreads and overall guilty look dragging along behind him, it was world war three up in our little studio apartment.

I accused him of being with Latonya, the college cutey he shared a graduate class with and was forever meeting at Starbucks or Barnes & Noble or after hours at the school library for so-called study sessions. On more than a few occasions his mistress had to be Angela, an older professional sister at his job who had a reputation for pouncing on younger professional brothers like himself, seducing them with promises that she could help move them up the corporate ladder because she knew the right people and could pull the right strings. Then there was his stalker ex-girlfriend Nikki from high school who followed him faithfully on every social media website known to man. Nikki was the same ex he admitted was still desperately in love with him which is why she liked all of his post and liked all of the pictures on his profile (except the ones with me in them), but while he claimed the feelings weren't mutual, being that he was adamant about not blocking her or deleting her from his friends list, it was obvious he enjoyed the attention.

A million dollars with my name on it would've said that whoever *she* was, *she* was a full blooded sister. A voluptuous, beautiful Black chick wrapped in skin the consistent tone and texture of black silk and walking in such smooth strides that if you weren't mistaken you'd look twice to make sure satin wasn't forming at the bottom of her heels. Surely, if he decided to take a walk on the wild side and risk his life and our marriage by cheating on me he had to have bet on black, right? Well wrong. Although painfully true, never in a million years would I have fathomed the idea of my man crossing the color line to swap bodily fluids with a White woman.

A White woman who was high enough to have the audacity to pick up my man's phone and between quick inhales, slow exhales, then a steady puff-puff of her weed, tell me she didn't care that he was married because he'd already told her all about me and according to him, it was my fault he was creeping around because I wasn't doing "my job".

Now she must've been holding the phone up and away from her ear because my husband's snores were so loud they echoed throughout the room and bounced off the walls picking up clearly through the receiver. There was no denying it, he was knocked out cold and oblivious that his little Caucasian plaything was playing on his phone, not only spilling the beans, but knocking the jar over all together. Blissfully asleep, this fool was oblivious to the fact that in exchange for the few minutes of heat they just shared, he had forfeited the rights to our four year marriage.

Coming back to the phone her high pitched squeaky voice cut through his heavy snoring and cut through my pride like a thousand rusty razors. "Heard that?" she asked in a snotty tone, "That's a sound you probably haven't heard in a long time, that's a satisfied man." She was a vicious and bold little White woman and even though she was sleeping with my husband and should've been apologizing ten times over for stepping out of bounds and into our marriage, instead she was intentionally trying to hurt me.

I could imagine a weak minded female such as herself easily being convinced by him that I was not only a horrible wife, but a horrible person overall. To absolve himself from any guilt of breaking the vows he made to me in front in God, family and friends, he had to make me out to be a nagging, contentious, unsupportive, unaffectionate, sneaky bitch who never cooked, let myself go in the looks department, didn't tend to or cater to him and was boring in the bedroom. With more lies, drama and plot twist than a Stephen King novel, I bet by the end of the his story she probably felt sorry for him and actually thought she was doing him a favor by being the sexy easy-going fling on the side, a distraction from a bad marriage.

With my man drooling all over her pillows there was no

denying that she had one up on me though and I could've matched her insult for insult, but I played it cool and decided to take the high road. What would be the point in sparing with a "woman" crazy enough, low enough, emotionally screwed up enough to think it was acceptable to brag about how skilled she was in sexually satisfying someone else's husband? What could be said to hurt her feelings when the coldhearted wench so obviously lacked any? What would I gain by lowering myself to her bottom of the barrel status by reducing my speech to the hot emotionally driven argument she was trying to draw me into. No matter how much I burned on the inside with fury, I would never allow myself to devolve into a ratchet wife. Side chicks, or what I call side dishes, even the uppity corporate ones thrive off of drama, yelling and the back and forth name calling. They so badly want to be the main girl or what I call the main course, but since they know they are only the scraps on the side; the cole-slaw, the potato salad, the red beans and rice, but never the filet mignon and probably won't ever be anything more than that, it makes them feel on your level if they pull you down to theirs.

I started laughing, which I guess threw her off, that in the midst of just discovering my dirty husband has a thing for dirty blondes I could find anything humorous about the situation, but I knew what she was trying to do. She could sit up there and have an argument with herself, I wouldn't be participating.

"Just let my soon to be ex-husband know that he doesn't have to bother coming home tonight because by the time he gets here his stuff will be packed in a bag for him and waiting outside on the porch with the rest of the trash," I said. Then added, "He was stinking up my house anyways."

"Sure bitch, I'll make sure to relay the message to your *soon to be ex-husband* when he wakes up," she scoffed, "but right now as you can hear, he's asleep."

Even though I maintained my composure for the most part, I let one insult slip and got loud on her for good measure, "Good, let sleeping dogs lie, but just remember *dummy*, when you lay down with dogs you can bet on catching fleas," I cautioned, but before she could start yapping again my finger landed squarely on the button shutting her up by hanging her up. And as much as I wanted to pretend that I was unaffected and unfazed by the fact that my man cheated on me with a woman who didn't even have a quarter of the class I possessed, but whose sole advantage was that her ancestors happened to crawl out the caves of Europe to establish their rule and reign over America, my body trembled and my heart pumped too fast to fake or front. Keeping it real, that call took away all my cool.

Before that day I used to cringe every time I saw a Black man hugged up with an Asian lady, kissing on a Hispanic chick or holding hands proudly walking down the street with a White woman. Cringe. The fine little hairs on the back of my neck would stand up straight, my chest would puff out ready to exhale all of my Black woman woes and I swear if I stared at them too long all happy and absorbed in each others crazy little mixed up world you could literally see the steam rising from the top of my head like they do in those cartoons. If I happened to make eye contact with one of these interracial lovers the expression on my face, which I couldn't hide, told of all my disgust and disapproval. That's why I would go out of my way not to look at them.

Before that day I could ignore them or simply turn the other cheek, but now they were at my doorstep, live, up close and very much personal. Dealing with the sticky residue of a marriage gone down the drain, sorting through bills, the lease and the like was one thing, but the emotional turmoil of my Black "brother" stepping over me to crown a Caucasian queen with his love and affection struck a chord so deep inside of me, hitting the pit of my stomach so hard that I literally felt sick.

Maybe I'm being overly dramatic, overly emotional, or overly sensitive, but I'm a Black woman living in a society where White men control a majority of the media, commercials, music videos, print ads and products that are all centered around White standards of beauty.

From time to time Black women do get their props, after all sisters have it going on and our beauty is hard for the world to ignore, but it's undeniable that when it comes down to first round draft picks in the mainstream, the White girl wins. The runner up to the White girl will be her closest imitator, the light skinned Black girl with long wavy hair or the rail thin Chinese chick whose eyes aren't that slanted or the Latina whose hair is blond, eyes sapphire blue with the only thing distinguishing her from any White woman is a slight olive skin tone and her last name which might be Lopez, Martinez, Garcia, or some other name with Spanish origins.

Brothers aren't blind either, they live here too. This ideology or what I call idiot-ology has been programmed in them since birth. From pre-school to grad school, Diapers to Depends they learn that the

White woman is to be treated as if she were royalty or a divine creature of beauty, splendor and desirability. She is considered as valuable and as precious as an expensive jewel, a cut above the rest, to be taken care of, provided for and protected at all cost.

And while the world bends its knee to the awe that is White women, Black women are left out in the cold, abandoned by our men and considered second class. Nobody even bats an eye to all the emotional beatings we have to endure on a daily basis or the stereotypes we have to constantly fight against. Stereotypes that paint us as fat, lazy welfare queens, hot tempered, loud, rude, jealous, promiscuous, angry, bitter Black women not worthy to be wives, but content with the label of baby mama when in reality most of us work or go to school or do both, are educated, attend church regularly, are in a monogamous relationship or longing for one, tithe, keep ourselves clean, pray, uplift one another and are happy, healthy and hardworking.

And while we are built beautifully, our bodies are shunned in the mainstream. We're taught to be ashamed of our brownie thick thighs, full-sized behinds and curves galore. They indiscreetly tell us to go on a diet, to drop the plate of mashed potatoes and cornbread in place of celery sticks and French vanilla slim-fast, to trade in our naturally nappy afros and cornrows for Brazilian weaves, to erase the chocolate hues in our skin with toxic hydroquinone laced skin lighteners. They have us bending over backwards to the point where our backs are breaking trying to mold ourselves into something we're not and won't ever be. Them.

Then at home a sister can't even rest from her woes because the very ones we're supposed to be able to come home to for sympathy and compassion after the world demeans us, the media tears us down or Hollywood shuns us, Black men, are off somewhere not only playing father, husband and lover to another, but often times bad mouthing us all the while too. So who do we have to turn to when our men turn their backs on us?

How are we to maintain strong Black families, promote and support healthy Black marriages and relationships between Black men and Black women when the rift is so wide and the ties that are supposed to bind us are so damaged that in a perpetual state of insanity a Black man will trade in his beautiful Black queen in which he shares a common history, common heritage and common destiny for a woman of another race he may have very little in common with?

How is that, when our beauty surpasses the beauty of billions of women? How is that, when from sea to shining sea and stretched out across several oceans there are many gorgeous colors, beautiful hues, and pretty shades, but Black is the most flawless of them all, an almost perfect tone envied by women all around the world? Women who in a frenzy to darken their complexions are caught sleeping in tanning booths, drenching themselves in tanning lotion or risking a serious bout with cancer by bathing in the sun, all to have what we are so blessed, yet so cursed to have, naturally sun kissed skin.

How is it that we're getting elbowed in the shoulder and pushed aside, told by our brothers that we're not good enough to date or marry? *Not good enough* when in the midst of all the pain we've endured, the overwhelming odds we've overcome, we've not only survived to raise their children with little or no help from them, but we made it seem almost effortless. When other women were cracking under the pressure of child rearing, drowning their kids in the bathtub, pulling their hair out and overdosing on prescription medications meant to treat their postpartum depression we stood tall, held our heads up, got knocked down and still got back up for more.

So then why are we deemed unworthy by so many of our men, while White women are held in such high regards? Why do some Black men see the icing on the cake of the American dream as marrying or making babies with a woman of a light or white skin tone? Where did this mindset come from and is the mental damage in accord with this thinking irreparable?

The answers go as far back as that time in history when Black people were dragged to this country kicking and screaming from the dirt hills of the continent of Africa. Those 400 years during which our folks were kidnapped from that torrid land, killed, tortured, raped and spread throughout the Caribbean and the Americas by Europeans who while doing these atrocities clapped their hands and sang 'Amazing Grace'.

We all know the story already. We know about the loss of languages, the separation of families, the dreadful exodus out of Africa and the awful passages to new lands that very few survived. The ones who did manage to endure the inhumane conditions of the transatlantic horror found themselves scattered in cold foreign terrain to endure centuries of enslavement so horrific that even though slavery existed for thousands of years before then, all over the world, and in almost every nation on earth, to use the term "slavery" automatically triggers thoughts of the African slave trade in most peoples minds.

Who hasn't heard about, read about or studied the dreadful fate that befell the African people? Who, raised in the public school system hasn't been on a school field trip to a museum and from behind a glass decorated with a *do not touch* sign, stared at a piece of broken rusty chain actually used to hold a human being captive centuries ago?

Slavery is a filthy, grimy, muddy smudge on what America would otherwise like to think of as its squeaky clean past. With lollipop sweet historical tales of pilgrims and puritans, forth of July and apple pie, slavery places a monkey wrench in the sugary cupcake accounts of this country's beginnings. Like a dead fly floating in a glass of expensive champagne, it just ruins the appeal. Run a background check on America and you'll find that while our so-called great "founding fathers" were demanding emancipation from England, crying out against tyranny and oppression, at that same time they were carrying out laws that allowed for the enslavement and oppression of Africans.

Some say, "Forget about it, all of that is in the past, stop dwelling on it," but Black people can no more forget slavery than Jews can forget the Holocaust. Unlike the chains of oppression that were loosened and ordered by law to be untied, slavery's psychological impact stuck like a filthy residue remaining long after the ink on the Emancipation Proclamation had dried.

Post slavery, America was the adopted home to roughly one million Africans. Shipping us back to the motherland would cause America's economic system to literally collapse, not to mention the social nightmare it would be for us because this is 400 years from when the enslavement of Black people first began, our languages are gone, our strong culture has been diluted and the memory of Africa is simply that, a memory. We don't know how to live over there because we've been here in North America for so long, so here we are to stay and here we are now "free".

Given enough time and enough love making we would surely multiply, outnumber the White race and take control of America. Despite our new found Christianity we might've even reversed the roles, bound them up in fetters and reciprocated some of the suffering they inflicted upon us. White people shivered at the possibility of what a suppressed people turned free could do in a position of power so with much planning and careful calculations they launched preemptive strikes against us to counter the probable attack. Slithering into the minds of an already weakened race of folks, White people got all up in our heads, rearranged our whole thinking and manipulated our very thought process.

They treated our people in such a way that made us believe we weren't worth the few dollars they paid for us even though in the majestic lands of Africa we hailed as kings and queens, reigned in dynasties, ruled empires, wore gold plates around our necks and in our ears, adorned our bodies with elaborate attire, garments and cloths woven out of the finest fabrics.

They made us dependent upon them for everything; food, water, clothes and shelter had to be given to us when they decided we needed it while back in Africa we provided for ourselves. We cultivated and harvested our own crops. African soil, like the womb of the women who inhabited the land, was fertile and brought forth an abundance of fruits and vegetables, coffee, teas and cocoa beans, sugar, spices, medicinal plants, precious metals, minerals and colorful gemstones. We fetched water from our own wells, stitched our own clothes, gathered sticks and mud and other building material from the earth and built our own homes, lived in them and lived content.

While Europeans credit themselves for great historical contributions to the civilized world and discredit Africans from any influence, Africans in fact mastered the sciences, made huge strides in mathematics, hailed as inventors and heavily influenced politics, religious practices, music, art and crafts worldwide. As a tremendously industrious continent, Africa became a huge trading partner with China and several Arab nations and African explorers navigated the treacherous seas to discover the goods of foreign lands, to the surprise and denial of many who defend the status quo, their explorations also included Europe and the Americas. Africa was not a disease riddled, starving, victimized, beggared continent with its hand held out for charity.

In Africa Africans toiled together reinforcing the principals of hard work, self-reliance and self-sufficiency, as well as collectivism, unity and brotherhood. We had the utmost respect for our elders, our men, our women and our young people. It didn't matter who we were, how light or dark our skin was, we belonged to each other and we looked out for one another. Basically in Africa, we had each other's back.

Here in America Whites turned Blacks against each other. They made us no longer trust one another, they made us envy one another and they made us no longer want to help each other or help ourselves for that matter. Our sole purpose from sun up to sun down was to work for Whites and help them build up wealth for themselves and their succeeding generations, while we lived dirt poor in shacks in the back of the plantation. So we wouldn't question their ruthless treatment of us or their authority and so we wouldn't get out of line, they beat the crap out of us and told us we deserved it because we were worthless, uncivilized, brainless, barbaric and too stupid to think or make decisions for ourselves.

They pitted the women against the men, the young against the old, the house "niggers" against the field "niggers" and the lighter skinned enslaved Africans against the darker skinned enslaved Africans. They divided us based on superficial differences, planted and then watered the seeds of self hatred within us, something we'd have to reap for generations to come.

With the White man convincing us of all these lies about ourselves, the institution of slavery could very well fall apart which it did, but harboring deep rooted feelings of self-hatred, distrust and contempt for each other meant it'd be difficult if not impossible to achieve any kind of unity amongst people of African descent. With perceptions of ourselves as inferior and inadequate ingrained in our souls, we had little to no chance of taking over the land of the so called free and home of the supposedly brave. So while we struggled, fought each other and engaged in activities certain to cause our own self-destruction, White people congratulated themselves, patted each others backs and exhaled as they were able to defend their notions of White superiority and supremacy over this great nation under God.

From then up until now a lot of Black folks have allowed themselves to be brain washed into believing everything that makes us unique and different from every other ethnicity on earth; the dark skin, kinky cotton textured hair, broad nose and full lips needed to be lightened, straightened, narrowed or thinned. Slavery is an open sore, a painful wound that's slow to heal and a scar Black people still carry with us because what happened way back then is still affecting so many aspects of our lives without us even being cognizant of its ramifications. While others just want us to get over it, unable to understand or tie what happened back then to what is going on right now, we're confined by the link.

At one point in time to see an interracial couple was like a hard slap in the face, a sting reminding me that while we've come far as a country, we really haven't come all that far as a people. That in 400 years despite freedom from slavery, the civil rights movement, Black panthers, Black power, Black is beautiful and a Black President, on occasion I can still slip into my figure flattering jeans, primp my hair in the mirror, walk out of the house fly, fresh and flawless with no make-up on except a dab of lip-gloss only to encounter more than few fools who while thinking they're giving me a compliment will tell me I'm pretty *for* a dark-skinned girl, as if pretty and dark-skinned wasn't synonymous.

"I usually don't date chocolate girls, but I'll make an exception for you since you're so fine," or "my type is light skinned with good hair, but since you got a nice booty, then hey what's up?" is what a lot of them will say somehow expecting me to jump for joy, flattered that they passed on girls who could win first prize in a Beyonce look-a-like contest for little'ole crispy black me. In this day in age by many Black men's standards dark skinned is too dark to be walked down the aisle, hand in hand while God, family, friends and other well wishers look on in pure happiness. They're scared to death of marrying and procreating with someone of a dark brown skin tone in fear that their children might come out resembling the little pickaninny children from those 1920's cartoons. You know those stereotypical little misfits whose hair stayed nappy, knobby knees stayed ashy, with huge lips used for gobbling down fresh summer watermelons.

This is what a lot of Black men dread, but seldom will admit because it is a form of self hatred. You see, to hate me is to hate yourself because like it or not I am your reflection, brother. If you're turned off by dark skinned women with kinky hair, but you look into the mirror everyday and see your own mahogany skin tone and your fingers get stuck trying to run them through your own nappy locks, then you are not comfortable with your own reflection. Brothers are quietly slipping on over to the white side thinking it's the right side, conveniently disguising their self-hatred and insatiable yearning for White America's acceptance with the phrase, "We just happened to fall in love and you can't control who you fall in love with."

I say you can control who you fall in love with and to fall in love with a woman with porcelain skin time and time again is not something stumbled upon by chance, but a well thought out calculated decision. And just for the record, White women don't steal our men, our men willingly and purposefully pursue them. Some brothers are cruising the internet going on interracial dating web sites specifically looking to chat with White women, seeking them out in bars, grinding on them on the dance floor at clubs frequented predominately by Whites, strategically seating themselves next to them in the cafeteria during lunch and showing up at hang out spots where they know White women will be only to say, they couldn't control who they fell in love with as if it happened by mistake.

Keeping it real, men never fall in love by mistake. They have to be in the right place in life, at the right time in their life, in the right frame of mind, and most importantly the woman they *decide* to fall in love with has got to be the right woman. Men and women are just different like that. While women are more picky about who we let slide up in us, and sloppy when it comes to who we fall in love with (think about how many times we've fallen in love and how many losers we've given our hearts to), men are just the opposite. They are careless when it comes to sex and will have it with just about anybody, but ultra selective when deciding who to fall in love with. It doesn't just happen. The saying goes, *women are ruled by their hearts and men are ruled by their parts.*

So for a man to fall in love, if it's the right time in his life, if he's achieved a certain level of success, if he's of a certain age and it's just time to start a family, he'll damn near plan it out from the moment he first meets a woman. From the way she's dressed to the way she carries herself a man plans on either taking her home tonight just for tonight, or plans on taking her home to momma.

The first thing he notices about her is how she looks; the style of her hair, the softness of her lips, the color of her skin, the size of her breast, the roundness of her behind, the narrowing of her waist against the widening of her hips, everything is going to get a once over and if she's attractive based on his predetermined ideas of beauty, a signal is sent from his brain to his southern region to get excited.

Now if he's been brainwashed by the constant bombardment of Eurocentric television images of anorexic looking stick thin waifish White women shoved down his throat everyday by the media, he might very well instantly reject a sister at first glance, finding her kinky hair, coffee brown skin and full figure size unpalatable. Stupid and confused because what should be his natural appetite for Black women is spoiled by the dominate culture and their monopoly on the beauty industry. He'll rather digest what he's been spoon fed all of his life.

After he determines that the physical features of a White or non-Black-close-to-White looking woman is pleasing to his eye, he then calculates what it takes to get her to be his, what it will cost him, what he'll have to give up, what sacrifices he'll have to make and will she be worth it. The buck doesn't stop there because in turn he's tallying up what benefits he'll gain from linking up with what the world considers as royalty, White women. He figures, as a Black man living in a world controlled by light skinned Asians, White Europeans, and White North Americans, his stock, which as a Black man is rather low, will somehow rise.

These same brothers weigh in their heads the pros and cons of hooking up with a sister and sadly enough many of them won't even approach us coming to the conclusion that a sister is simply not worth the effort. That's why Black women roll our eyes because we know all of this is being consciously or unconsciously juggled around in a brother's mind at first sight. While we're being stereotyped and prejudged from the jump, a White…Asian…Latina girl is automatically given credit, skin credit. Before she even opens her mouth to introduce herself brothers are already picturing the easy, stress free, non-drama filled, comfortable life they'll have with her and what they stand to gain from such a union. So when most Black men marry or date outside of their race and say it's because they just so happen to fall in love, we know what the real deal is.

Sometimes it's the end result of their dissatisfaction and disgust for Sisters. Brothers don't like to admit to it, but in those hush-hush moments off the record, off camera with the microphone unplugged and with the lights dimmed I've overheard them saying they've given up on Black women. One real amazing sister they may have granted their heart to way back when trampled over it with her Jimmy Choos stomping it into a bloody pulp, crushing it and his chance of ever loving another Black woman in the process. One Black woman breaks a brothers heart or has a rank attitude or digs the gold out of his pockets leaving behind nothing but lint and he immediately stereotypes all of us into that same category, ready to throw in the towel and give up on all of us when in contrast we've suffered heart break after painstaking heart break at the hands of Black men only to brush the dirt off of our shoulders and love their rusty black butts again. We might be a little insecure in the next relationship at first due to what the last man did, but sure enough we'll give the new man a chance anyway and let him prove that all Black men aren't the same.

Unfortunately some brothers aren't as forgiving, there you

have the Black men who date White women exclusively. Black women are completely crossed off the list and the White girl they get with next has to hear about how difficult we were to deal with, how we weren't fulfilling their physical or emotional needs, how they can't stand us because we have attitudes, we didn't do this, refused to do that, blah, blah, blah.

They shouldn't get away with rejecting a whole race of women without being called racists, because let's call a spade a spade, any Black man who refuses to associate with Black women is a stone cold bigot. Some race trading, self hating, Uncle Tom hiding out in the big house was too busy trying to erase the melanin in his skin to acknowledge his own self-hatred and decided his reason for creeping with the master's wife was somehow a Black woman's fault. That we were somehow responsible for his actions by not doing our "job" or fulfilling his "needs" or falling in line with his chauvinistic European ideas of femininity. Just fueling a sister's insecurities.

Many "brothers" after him have followed suit, insistent on blaming their crossing the color line on Black women. They've thrown out reasons like we're moody, loud mouthed and belligerent and have accused us of having bad attitudes, but breaking it down all that means is that a Black woman won't put up with any of his crap. We'll call a brother out on his mess, hold him accountable for his foolishness and we aren't the least bit scared to speak our minds. That's the one thing about Black women, we're brutally honest. Like it or not you can always bet a Black woman is going to tell it like it is, give it to you straight no chaser.

From the smacking of our lips, down to the extra switch in our hips, to the acrylic fingertips that complement the firmness of our grip, yeah, sisters are sassy. Not to be confused with being a bitch because on the flip we'll still take care of our men. A sister will be up in the kitchen cooking for her man, holding the household together, out there slaving 12 hour shifts when times get rough and for whatever reason he can't do it, having her mans back in every and anyway possible and still manage to look flawlessly beautiful in the process.

A real brother admires the boldness of our ways, is practically intoxicated with our mixture of feistiness, confidence and the spice we add to his life and because he enjoys the challenge, the chase and the sexy strength of a Black woman, he's going to have our back too. A real brother might even witness his heart rate accelerate, finding that a complex Black woman is a turn on in ways that make any other woman seem bland or boring in comparison.

On the other hand a weak "brother" will sink insecurely in his seat, he'll whimper the moment we start demanding, requiring or asking questions of him and not wanting to be challenged he might run for refuge in a relationship with another woman. If anyone happens to ask why he isn't sporting any dark and lovely ladies on his arm, to save his manhood and so as to not seem like a wimp he'll lie and say it's because Black women have attitudes.

If I had a dime for every time my ears were polluted with that *Black women have attitudes* garbage I'd have more than enough money to buy some of these "brothers" who say it some sense. The world already unfairly perceives Black women to be mean, angry or attitudinal without our own men reiterating the stereotype. In reality women by nature are emotional creatures so Black, White, Brown, Yellow, Red, we all have attitudes. At certain times of the month when our hormones are kicking into overdrive we all get, what some might consider a little mean or a little crabby. While our bodies adjust to the hormonal changes the sour mood is just nature's way of allowing us to release some steam so that it won't build up and drive us crazy. Black women in particular have a lot more steam to let go since we go through a lot more.

The average Black woman is dealing with things on a daily basis that most men and women of other races couldn't even fathom having to deal with. Hair issues, body issues, self-esteem issues, indiscreet racism, single parenthood, rejection from our own men, having too much independence to the point of loneliness up there on the top by ourselves. Sometimes the stress, strain, pressure and anxiety in the everyday life of a Black woman comes out as anger or what our society likes to call an attitude, but when we hurt we scream, when we're upset we don't tuck it away, we show it. Granted some of us need to learn how to show it in more appropriate ways at more appropriate times, but for the most part, good or bad we wear our emotions on our sleeves.

Yes, there are some difficult Black women out there who give the rest of us a bad rap; arrogant, ignorant, loud, rude, overly aggressive, confrontational and more interested in the size of a brothers bank account and the size of his penis, than the size of his heart, but for the most part the majority of us are misunderstood.

Could it be that we constantly have to prove our beauty and our self worth because for years society and the media has made every attempt possible to ignore our beauty, teach us to be ashamed of it, disguise it or dismiss it altogether? Could it be that we're stuck having to raise the children by ourselves that Black men left behind so they could in fact go be with White women? Could it be that we're forced to be the breadwinner, the HNIC because too many of our men can't, won't, or don't have the means necessary to provide for us?

Could it possibly be that Black women are confronted with shocking statistics that say we're the least likely among all races of women to ever get married, although ironically most of us will experience the indescribable delight of giving birth? Too many of us will have to live our love lives vicariously through one of our girlfriends, who happened to be lucky enough to beat the odds and find a man who wanted to do more than just get down in the bedroom, but actually wanted to get down on one knee.

Could it be that most of us are in a perpetual state of panic as we watch our men practically disappear around us, while the remainder of us have our claws out, sharpened, and on constant defense because we're fighting for the few good ones that are left? Black women have had to fight our whole lives, put up with too much mess not to have an attitude, but it's not attitude we're showing, it's a potent blend of hormones and frustration.

The tripped out part about it is Black men are frustrated too. Black men have been fighting their whole lives too. Fighting some invisible battles we Black women can't see or even begin to understand. Battles with their self-worth, self-esteem, identity, masculinity, and their role in society. While White women are the standard Black women are constantly being measured by when it comes to beauty, sexual conduct and character, White men set the financial and socio-economic standards Black men are compared to. And just like us, according to society, Black men often times fall short in the comparison.

All they have to do is open up their eyes to see that White men control and dominate most of the systems of the world. "The man" formulates the laws Black men have to abide by and are often times discriminated against with. After all, who governs political organizations, presides over most of the legal systems, controls the judicial courts and is in charge of the police force? White men. Subsequently, who fills up the majority of America's jails and prisons? Black men. Who owns most of the land, businesses, oil, energy and resources that Black men and Hispanic immigrants are paid low wages to build, till, tend and cultivate? White men. They hook up their unqualified fresh-out-of-college-no-job-experience-whatsoever nephews and their incompetent never-been-to-college son-in-laws with jobs a Black man might spend half his life building up his resume for. It is still an ugly little reality that a Black man with a sparkling clean background will have a harder time finding a job than a White man with a felony conviction on his criminal record.

At every turn it's apparent that White men have the money, the power, and the worlds' respect. The only way some Black men see themselves as powerful or controlling anything is in relationships and through sex. Brothers are strutting around with their chests puffed out, trying to be players, cocky with their arrogance on full blast, emasculated by America and concealing their insecurities by dating White women. Women who they think might be easier to manipulate and control and who they think will worship the ground they walk on, thus giving them the worthiness, recognition and respect denied by society.

Because when a White woman is blessed with the companionship of a Black man she might very well treat him better than she treated any of her previous White lovers. The White woman who can get a hold of a Black man's heart is a woman who knows she's got a lot of responsibility and will have to work hard not to lose his interest. Dating back to polygamous tribes in Africa, historically speaking Black men don't exactly have a reputation for monogamy, and better believe White women are well aware of this.

What they're also aware of is how discriminated against Black men are by White men. Some White women grew up in homes where their fathers, uncles and older brothers repeatedly spewed racist remarks about Black people (Black men in particular) and didn't hesitate to let their daughters, nieces and little sisters know that these *lazy, drug dealing, gang-banging, multiple baby-mama-having niggers* weren't good enough for them. And that they better not ever bring them home unless they wanted to be disowned by the family.

White women know the stereotypes better than we know them. So a lot of them work overtime pumping their boyfriends' heads up with how freaking wonderful they are, how much they adore them and how they, not the White man, are the kings of the freaking universe. The real Mandingo. With just a few compliments White women know how to take a down trodden Black man and make him feel like an A-class world champion. Now because she's spent all of her time building him up, praising him, transforming him into a demigod, she'll tip-toe around his ego, careful not to step on it. Often times she won't challenge him when he's wrong or put him in his place when he's stepped out of line, but may very well forget the whole feminist movement and bow down submissively in the presence of the almighty black penis.

Some White men hate to see Black men with their women too for this very reason. They seethe at the sight of young beautiful White women who won't even give them the time of day sacrificing their dignity by throwing themselves at high profile professional Black athletes, or even the tatted up thugs on the corner. There's an underlying anger felt by White men bubbling just below the surface that plays into their self-esteem as well, but it never surfaces. It's just not politically correct or socially acceptable for a White man to voice his concerns. The NAACP would be hot on his trail, so he keeps quiet, reserving his "racist" remarks for internet chat rooms and blogs where he can maintain his anonymity.

A Black woman on the other hand, humph! As said before, a sister doesn't hold her tongue for anything or anybody and is sure enough going to make her displeasure known out loud. The neck twist, the fed up eye rolls, the cold stares, the long drawn out sighs Black women make when we see a fine Black man drooling over a not so fine White women is born out of very painful feelings. We are not trying to present ourselves as angry attitudinal miserable haters who mope through life with a permanent chip on our shoulders. These stereotypes about us and the daunting statistics we face are just what come to mind when we see a Black man/White woman interracial couple. We know that for every White Woman who's safely cuddled up at night with a financially stable Black man and is being told how beautiful she is while he runs his fingers through her silky hair, there's a smart, beautiful, sweet Black woman who's all alone.

There are endless explanations for why Black men date outside of their race, but I genuinely believe when you put us together in this melting pot of races and cultures and ethnicities and languages that makes America so beautiful there will always be a natural mixing. Every day in malls, bookstores or standing in line at the grocery store I see interracial couples. Blacks and Hispanics, Whites and Asians, Asians and Latinos, Blacks and Whites, Latinos and Whites, Blacks and Asians, the rainbow is fabulous. I've seen every ethnicity on earth embraced in love, but you can't tell me the scale isn't a little off balance and there aren't more Black men mixing with White women than any other two races and genders. Just like you can't tell me that when it comes to successful, athletically accomplished or financially well-off suit and tie brothers the numbers aren't even higher.

I'm flipping through the TV stations and bam there it is. A handsome gorgeous big strapping dark chocolaty professional brother is doing an interview on how he got his business started, they'll cut away to a shot of his family and there is his White wife smiling all up in the camera with their little biracial kids cheesing all up in the camera too. I flip the station again and now I see a famous Black movie star walking the red carpet at the premier of his new blockbuster film and who's hanging on his arm? You guessed it, a White woman. A couple channels down on ESPN there's Mr. MVP, who just won another Super bowl ring or Championship trophy and the woman celebrating by his side looks nothing like the Black chicks from his old neighborhood who used to cheer him on at those high school games, back before he turned pro, back when he used to play in beat up old sneakers because his money was funny and that's all he could afford.

Nothing can match the betrayal we feel when the very men we nurture, love and support during their times of struggle suddenly strikes a little bit of fortune or fame and decides that we're no longer good enough to have that nurturing loving support reciprocated. How many sisters have stood by a brother's side when he was broke, couldn't find a job, living at home with his momma, struggling trying to make it, didn't have a car and was catching the bus only to watch him graduate from college, land that six figure salary corporate job, start his own business, sign that recording contract or that basketball contract, then suddenly act like he doesn't even know a sisters name. Suddenly he has money and no longer attracted to Black women, suddenly we're too much to handle, he doesn't want to deal with us anymore and a White woman is the one curling his toes at night.

This type of successful brother is too infatuated with the American dream to wake up and realize that some of those White women are only down for him because times are smooth, the bottles are popping, the spotlight is shining, and there's constant cash flow. But I wonder if some of those brother embezzling White women would be willing to move out of the mansions, give up their diamonds and furs or part with any of the worldly possessions they've been blessed with by their Black men if his knee happened to get injured in a game and he could no longer play or his movies tanked at the box office or his businesses straight ran out of business. I wonder how many of those lovely White women successful brothers can't get enough of would stick around to see them fade from the limelight, have their cars repossessed or luxurious homes foreclosed on or worse have to turn back to eating beef flavored Ramen noodles because filet mignon is no longer in the budget.

Is she still going to be down or is she going to buy a one way ticket out of town to catch the next thing smoking? Brothers are playing themselves if they think the type of White woman they could *only* get after they made it to the top will do anything less than leave their sorry behinds behind, buried in debt and drowning in a pile of past due bills. Yet and still we see Black men tripping over each other in a race to dip their hands into the White man's cookie jar, trampling us in the process.

But as much as Black women are tired of being trampled on, tired of being passed over, tired of being talked negatively about, tired of being overlooked by Black men and tired of being overshadowed by White women, the majority of us don't believe interracial relationships are intrinsically bad, we just understand the motive behind the relationship sometimes can be. In fact, many of us are in strong advocates of love in any size, shape or color. We're staunch defenders of anything that remotely looks like it because there's so very little of it in the world today. I won't hate on anybody who's truly in love because love is the most wonderful gift God has given us next to life itself, but I strongly believe in Black love. Take two people who share the same pain, the same struggles, the same culture, the same history and the same destiny and the chemistry is explosive.

But yes, admittedly at one point in time I used to cringe when I saw a Black man hugged up with an Asian lady, kissing on a Puerto-Rican chick or holding hands proudly walking down the street with a

White woman. Cringe. The fine little hairs on the back of my neck would stand up straight, my chest would puff out ready to exhale all of my Black woman woes and I swear if I stared at them too long all happy and absorbed in each others crazy little mixed up world you could literally see the steam rising from the top of my head like they do in those cartoons. If I happened to make eye contact with one of these interracial lovers the expression on my face, which I couldn't hide told of all my disgust and disapproval. That's why I would go out of my way not to look at them.

Well, that was a long time ago. I'm secure enough now to hold my head up high, look them directly in the eyes, maybe even smile and not take their love for one another as a personal assault. It's hard, and as tempted as I am to join some of my fellow sisters in the public chastisement of interracial lovers, I know I'm above all of that pettiness; the turning up my nose, making snide little rude comments, being disrespectful to couples just minding their business on the street. I'm better than that. We're all better than that. And that, well that's what makes Black women so special, so strong. We've been getting pushed down, torn down, talked down to, been down on our luck and down and out, but in the legacy of the late Dr. Maya Angelou, still we rise.

So with the grace and guile only befitting of a queen, I smile. On a rare occasion the brother might even smile back and out of the corner of his eye, unbeknownst to his Caucasian companion he might hold a stare just a tad too long. Admiring the curve of my backside, twisted up in the fancy braids decorating my hair, seduced by the sway of my hips, hypnotized by the harmony of my skin tone with his skin tone, my strong African bone structure and all. Oh the sweet blessings he surrendered for what he might've thought was a better shot at the American dream.

In America, Black men have the freedom to chase the dream, and the right to choose who they date, who they marry and who they make their pretty little babies with. Brothers, just don't do it at the expense and insult of Black women. Don't tell me you don't want to date me because I'm not attractive enough, mean, attitudinal, too strong or too black. Don't defend your love or lust for White women and women of other races by saying I'm too this or I'm not enough of that. Take responsibility for your own choices and be man enough not to blame your preference for White women and women of other races on what you think are the shortcomings of Black women. Just remember who nursed you when you were sick, lent you money when you were broke and whose smile has brightened your life when you faced your darkest days. Think about these things before turning your back on a whole race of women who look like the woman whose breast nurtured you when you were young. Acknowledge that through the blessings and grace of God a Black woman gave you life and express gratitude by uplifting the lives of your sisters.

Rated "R" for Rap
generation hip-hop

In my opinion the majority of hip-hop music out today and the culture that goes along with it has gone way too far. It's Saturday night and I'm smack dab in the middle of the dance floor shaking what my momma gave me just having a good time with some friends. Three fly females looking like we just stepped out of the pages of Black Glamour magazine. Make-up, done to perfection. Nails, French tipped with toes painted candy apple red. Hair, curled, bumped, spritzed, oil-sheened, and shining. Heels, so high our legs look as if they lead straight up to heaven. "Only You" an old skool collaboration by 112, Mase and Biggie is flooding out of the speakers giving everybody a music induced high when all of a sudden the song switches up to another collab from the nineties called "Freak Hoes" by Master P, Silkk the Shocker and Mia X.

We're dancing while "Freak Hoes" is playing so what do we look like in the center of the club? After a while we become the center of attention as guys start backing up, making a circle around us like we're the hired entertainment or in some kind of freak circus. Before I become a freak hoe in a freak show I'm sorry, but I'm sitting this one out. On my way to find a seat the song switches up again, this time to something with even more vulgar lyrics than the previous song, something along the lines of "Drop it Bitch". I don't even know who the song is by, but at this point it doesn't matter, I am too through. My arms are folded and my nose is pointed up while my eyes are looking down on all the other girls who in the name of good fun are dropping down low making their knees touch their elbows.

Later on that night after 'I'm a pimp', 'shake dat' ass', 'make it rain on them hoes', 'hoe this', 'bitch that', 'bend over', 'gimme some head', 'spread them legs' and 'slide down the pole' I'm hiding in a corner sipping down the last of my Grey Goose and cranberry juice when a skinny J.J. Evans looking brother who says he spotted me earlier dancing with my friends comes over and asks me to show him some more of my moves. Until the D.J. planned on playing something decent I could very well have sat right there until my friends were ready to go so I politely decline his request.

Not like I was interested in getting close to him anyway. Brother man looked hungry, malnourished is the word, and I was about to start going around collecting donations so they could feed the needy. He was wearing a dingy short-sleeve white T-shirt and oversized washed out blue jeans, which were sagging off of his boney butt like a mud slide, showing off a pair of dirty looking boxer shorts. On top of that a tear drop tattoo graced his upper cheek just below his bloodshot red eyes and a lone gold tooth shined all bright in its glory as he tried to persuade me to get up and dance with him. Once again I politely turn down his offer.

But brothers are persistent as hell because now we're on this back and forth tip. He's basically begging for a dance and I'm basically begging to be left alone, but he refuses to take no for an answer. Bag of bones is obviously drunk because he grows more aggressive, grabs my hand pulling me to my feet, squeezes me close enough to where I can feel a small (*emphasis on small*) bulge in his pants and smell the stench of his breath heavily perfumed with weed and rum.

I jerk back as if he's a leper, gives him an evil up and down stare that speaks for itself, "back away unless you want to get slapped away" and when he hesitates I use my forearms to push him out of my space. Behind him, a group of sisters swinging their hips to the music lose their groove and cuss up a storm as his drunk tail stumbles into them, spilling drinks, stepping on toes. "My bad, damn," I hear him apologizing to the angry weave wearing crew of girls, and as I'm fleeing the scene he shouts loud enough for me to also hear his voice clearly over the music calling me a stuck up bitch. Well I'll be a stuck up, uptight, high sadity, bougie bitch before I disgrace myself, disrespect my gender, or disregard my beliefs by dancing to any song that glorifies the sexual exploitation of women.

This is the respect I get for trying to respect myself, but then again this is generation Hip-hop and in generation Hip-hop instead of having respect for ourselves and each other, basically it's *I don't give a Fuck. Fuck the police, fuck the law, fuck school, fuck you and if your momma's in the way fuck your momma too. Family values? Fuck the family. Love? Fuck love, love is a bitch and bitches ain't shit. Modesty, humility, unity? Fuck all dat, it's all about me and what I can get and if I have to step on you to get it, consider yourself stepped on. Respect? We don't give a fuck, remember.*

I guess we would like to forget where rap music originated. That its roots were founded in unity and respect, not chaos and disregard for values or morality. The loud pulsating beats came thumping out of Africa, the motherland as a reflection of our expressive, sassy and sultry culture. The drums and the bass and all the variety of instruments were hand crafted to create sounds as hypnotic and seductive as they were wild. Once those African hands got to pound those drums, nothing with a spirit or an ear could sit still. Like a chow bell signaling it was time to eat, those instruments signaled it was time to celebrate, worship and dance. Isn't that what we hear today in our historically Black college and university marching bands? Isn't that what we hear on Sunday mornings from our Black churches and in our places of worship? Africa is the origin.

Fast forward a few years and those beats along with every other precious African creation have now been pick pocketed by Europeans, but what's left of the rhyme pattern has evolved, merged with Rhythm and Blues, funk, Jamaican dub music, soul, disco and other forms of music derived from Africa, and somehow landed in the gritty streets of New York. A few Black inner-city youths discover they can rhyme short impromptu poetry-like versus over the beats played by Disc Jockeys and there you have it. Pop the champagne, light a cigar, send out the announcements, hip-hop is born.

Late seventies and early to mid-eighties hip-hop started out as a cultural mixture of party music fused with social commentary. On one side you had the break dancing, beat-boxing brothers rocking thick gold rope chains, kangol hats, track suits and Adidas to block parties and house parties. While on the other side the zealous lyrics of fighting the power, Black power and power to the people ignited a socially conscious community of raised fist and necks adorned with red, green and black medallions in the shape of the African continent. We were getting our party on, having fun and at the same time being schooled on principals of Black Nationalism, Black unity and Black empowerment.

Then, in the time it took to snap our fingers to the beat, just like that the tides had shifted. Gone were the good old days of power and unity because nineties hip-hop became a lethal blend of misogyny and gangsta rap. 2-Live Crew was telling girls to 'pop that coochie' while N.W.A. was yelling, 'fuck tha police'. The majority of the music was either glorifying gangsta life; selling drugs, gang banging, violence and incarceration, or promoting the pimp and hoe lifestyle; sex and money, more sex and more money. Gold-digging girls using their bodies as sexual objects to trick dumb brothers into handing over all their material possessions, and dumb brothers flaunting their material possessions like their cars, their jewels and their houses to get sex.

Years later not much has changed. If anything it's gotten worse, raunchier, more vulgar and viler. At least back then we had community organizers, religious leaders and Black politicians like Al Sharpton, Jessie Jackson and Delores Tucker and them out on the forefront protesting the filth in our music, because today it seems like no one cares to even bat an eyelash. We just kind of leave it alone because hip-hop just seems too culturally relevant, too profitable, too big to fight. Like that bully on the playground who's been held back in the same grade twice so he's bigger than the other kids, angry all the time, punking people for their lunch money. He's popular and you're considered cool if you play with him and so you play with him, but deep down inside none of the kids really like him because they know he's bad, but then again they're kinda fascinated by him for the same reason. Yeah, hip-hop is like that oversized bully, we'll play with him because he's fun, but everybody's afraid to mess with that kid.

Years back though, we had everybody jumping down radio shock jock Don Imus' throat for calling some basketball girls nappy headed hoes. He received a public beheading at the hands of Black folks. Don Imus is old, White, and irrelevant to most young Black people. Most young Black people didn't even listen to Don Imus, let alone know who he was before all the controversy, but his old wrinkled self was all over the news, all over the internet, and was the subject of talk shows and blogs. Black people chased him out of town with torches and pitch forks, wanted his head on a silver platter, wanted to hang him without a trial and due process. As stupid and insensitive as his comments were, I could care less what Don Imus said because you know what, young Black boys are not listening to Don Imus, but they're smoking weed, letting their jeans sag, talking in slang, and professing to be pimps just like *what's-his-name-fill-in-the-blank,* whoever's the hot rapper of the season.

So today I'm dressed in all black, mourning the souls of Black men, particularly young Black men who are dearly departing from our lives spiritually because they've allowed raunchy lyrics to sink into their subconscious, manipulate their behavior and control their thoughts and desires. I'm crying for young Black men who are listening to rap music, watching the videos, emulating what they hear, imitating what they see and forming their opinion of women, of life and how they are to treat themselves and others. Weeping over young Black men who grow up without daddies, who because they belong to generation hip-hop does not have enough strong Black male role models to look up to like they did in the Civil Rights era so are idolizing rich rappers and wealthy ball players. Rappers who spend more time in jail than they do in the studio and athletes who spend more time in court than they do on the court.

What's supposedly censored and playing on any given hip-hop radio station across America at any given time of the day is literally murdering and mutilating their spirits. The microphone has become a deadly weapon used to slay our men and rap music, the mass grave in which to bury their dead and dying souls. As opposed to dying physically, spiritual death occurs slowly over time, is far more painful and dulls the soul making it unable to relate to anything beyond the tangible or material level. A dead soul wonders around aimlessly making feeble attempts to attain love, peace of mind, fulfillment, joy or contentment by participating in destructive behaviors and pursuing empty things, but always comes up short because there is no love, peace of mind, fulfillment, joy or contentment apart from God.

While parents were too busy paying the bills and having a social life, while our church leaders were baking brownies for the bake sale and raffling off flat screen T.V.'s to fund the new building project, pop culture snuck in stealing the strong influence these forces once held on our community. With inner city school districts cutting funds for after school programs and extra-curricular activities, a lot of our children come home after school to empty apartments with too much time on their hands. White people call them latchkey children, but we don't have any special names for them because in the Black community a majority of our children are raised by single mothers who don't have the luxury of being housewives so are at work in the afternoon leaving their children unsupervised for hours at a time. After Cheetos, chocolate milk and everything else laden with sugar, trans fats, preservatives and artificial colors many of these "latchkey" children plop their behinds down in front of the TV for vulgar video games, lewd sitcoms and dramas or BET's top ten countdown.

Guns, drugs, blood and sex are commercially manufactured into young minds on the daily. As soon as they drop their backpacks, like an all out attack against their innocence they're bombarded by a hailstorm of deplorable images and messages. A child who hasn't yet acquired the maturity to process fantasy from reality without an adult around to explain and differentiate the real from the fake is likely to act out on his own interpretation of whatever it is he's seeing or hearing. Kindergarteners are carrying concealed handguns to school to show off to their friends and fifth graders are stealing and selling their parents prescription meds to other classmates. Six grade girls are giving head in the boys bathroom stall between classes and six grade boys are molesting their female classmates under the bleachers in the gym. Ninth grade girls are using their allowance money to buy pregnancy tests and ninth grade boys are using their allowance money to buy condoms.

Our children's morals can be summed up by the lyrics of the top ten songs on the billboard charts, yet the mentality of our community is, *'if the song has a good beat turn it up, that's my jam, turn it up a little louder please'*. The attitude of most entertainers, especially rappers is, *'as long as I'm getting paid'* or *'I rap, I sing, I do my thing, but I'm not a role model.'* I wish rappers weren't role models, but unfortunately for too many of our kids they are.

If entertainers only understood the power they have. If they truly realized the tight grasp they hold on an entire generation. If for one moment they could hop off their high horses, take a break from being worshipped by their legions of fans, and possibly float back down to reality where us mere mortals reside, they'd then realize that their music has the power to manipulate minds, positively inspire or negatively influence millions of impressionable young people who will one day be running this country, resulting in the reshaping of a whole culture.

Proverbs 18:21 says, "Death and life are in the power of the tongue...," but let these rappers tell the story and since they're getting praised, paid, and promoted their tongues are not at fault for the physical or spiritual deaths of our young men and young women. You hear rappers complaining on TV that they're used as scapegoats for everything that goes wrong among Black youth, that every time a child lashes out in violence the finger is automatically aimed at the music. Since they didn't bring drugs or guns or poverty into the Black community, rappers believe they aren't responsible for the house riddled with bullets next door from last night's drive-by, or Ms. Johnsons 16 year old son being robbed and murdered on his way home from basketball practice, or 14 year old Tameka Thompson getting pregnant by a man twice her age.

According to them, slavery, institutionalized racism, corrupt government officials and failed government policies are to blame for the ills of the Black community, which existed long before they ever picked up a microphone. Their music, they claim, is simply a mirror of the chaos already going on in the Black community, not the cause of it. Rappers pout and point to parents, politicians, and policemen refusing to acknowledge that although these things are to blame, they themselves share a heaping slice of the charge as well.

Just because rappers aren't the only ones causing corrosion to the Black community doesn't mean we shouldn't hold them accountable, because they are part contributors and co-conspirators in its downward spiral. To inspire this *I'm-going-to-fuck-5-or-6-hoes, then-go-home-to-my bitch, put-my-chrome-to-your-dome-and-blast-your-ass, bust-your-head-wide-open-because-nigga-I-don't-give-a-fuck* attitude makes them just as guilty of the physical, mental, and spiritual death of our people as Klansmen in the old south who hung our men from trees while our women watched in horror knowing they were next in line to be raped.

How ignorant can we be to look at what the White man has done to us all these years with the whips and chains, the dogs and the hoses, the cross burnings on our lawns and setting our churches on fire and call him a racist, yet turn right on around and allow our entertainers to do the same thing to us figuratively while we happily pay them to do it. We'll be all up in the audience at their concerts clapping, and dancing, and waving our hands in the air like we just don't care, while they're up on the stage calling us niggas and bitches. Here it is, over a century since our ancestors shook off the shackles of slavery embracing their new found freedom, years after segregation signs were painted over in new ink welcoming anyone on in to eat and long after we stopped singing we shall overcome because hell, we've already overcome, but Black people are still being dogged, degraded, and disrespected by our own people in our own music.

Female rappers are chanting, "Get that niggas dough," and the men are screaming back, "She ain't nothing but a gold digging hoe," back and forth like who can dog who out the worst. Our sisters are singing about each other's cheap nappy weave, so-and-so's inability to keep a man, how she took her man and proclaiming themselves to be the baddest bitch while our brothers are battling to be the best rapper breathing by dissing each other's rhymes, bragging about having sex with someone else's hoe, and stirring up some fake manufactured beef to sell more records.

Communication between Black men and Black women wasn't always this vulgar and rough and rude. It wasn't always about stealing somebody's man or beating somebody's ass or getting somebody to perform oral sex on you during a one night stand after the club. Those things went on amongst Black folks, but it surely wasn't celebrated, smiled upon, or sung about in our music. See, our music was our refuge, our hiding place, our sanctuary. A pretty place we could pack away our troubles and visit whenever the world around us got ugly. And ugly, it was more often than not. See, there was enough negativity outside the music; racism, poverty, police brutality, that when the music started playing we wanted to forget all of that, get lost in the lyrics, hide in the harmony, wrap ourselves in the rhythm, be a part of the beat, find salvation in the song. The last thing we wanted to hear was a Black man calling himself or another Black man a nigger, or a Black woman calling herself or another Black woman a bitch, or vice-versa.

In the sixties the Temptations sung their way to the top of the charts and into the hearts of millions of women with the catchy hit, "The Way You Do the Things You Do" and had sunshine on a cloudy day with, "My Girl". No woman could resist the smooth velvety voice of Smoky Robinson crooning, "Ooo Baby, Baby" and there had to be a spike in the birth rate after "Cruisin", with lyrics like, "...*if you want it you got it forever, [this is not a one night stand]...I could just stay there inside you and love you*". The ladies as well had a voice for love with the Supremes singing, "Baby Love", "Stop in the Name of Love", and "You can't Hurry Love" while Aretha Franklin supplied fuel for the feminist movement by demanding "R-E-S-P-E-C-T".

When divorce and broken homes started to become the norm in the Black community, Al Green took the seventies by storm with, "Let's Stay Together" inspiring couples to stick it out *whether times are good or bad, happy or sad*" with "Love and Happiness" following suit. Jermaine Jackson declared that, "Daddy's Home", Sly and the Family Stone said "It's a Family Affair", and Sister Sledge made it known that "We Are Family". Then, when gangs and crime and drugs began to overtake inner cities, Marvin Gaye's socially conscious hit "What's Going On?" caused the whole nation, fresh off its battle for civil rights and crippled by stories and images of the Vietnam war, to pause and wonder just that.

Even as rap and hip-hop rose to fame, themes of love in Black music climaxed in the nineteen-eighties and dominated the decade. In the eighties, practically every Black couple who got married had Atlantic Starr's classic wedding ballad "Always" playing at their reception along with "You are My Lady" by Freddie Jackson, "Endless Love" by Diana Ross and Lionel Richie and "Here and Now" by Luther Vandross. Speaking of Luther Vandross, he's probably responsible for getting millions of couples to the altar with, "A House is Not a Home", "So Amazing", "If Only for One Night" and the cover of Marvin Gaye and Tammi Terrell's "If This World Were Mine" among countless other sweet soulful songs.

Then there was the mellow whistle of the harmonica in Gregory Abbott's "Shake You Down", Gerald Levert telling his woman he'd get down on his knee for her in "Casanova", the Isley Brothers making love "Between the Sheets", piano rendition or acapella version of Stevie Wonder's "Ribbon in the Sky", Sade's lush romantic British accent fused with the groovy quiet storm vibe creating the "Sweetest Taboo", "Whip Appeal" by BabyFace", "Nite and Day" by Al B. Sure, "Sweet Love" by Anita Baker, "All I do is Think of You" by Troop, "Tender Love" by Force M.D., "Make it Last Forever" by Keith Sweat…the list goes on and on and on.

And please let's not forget about New Edition, all their chart toppers and number ones and all the Spin-off talent that group produced. Ralph Tresvant, Johnny Gill, Bel Biv DeVoe, LSG, Heads of State, even bad boy Bobby Brown displayed his softer side with eighties hits, "Roni", "Rock Wit'Cha" and "Every Little Step".

In addition to all the lovey-dovey panty dropper mushy music out at the time, messages of friendship, brotherly love, and humanitarianism resonated throughout eighties music as well. Michael Jackson's, "Man in the Mirror" challenged each individual to take a look at themselves in order to change the world, Lionel Richie and friends raised funds for African hunger relief with "We Are the World", Dionne Warwick sung "That's What Friends Are For" in lieu of World AIDS day and Whitney Houston's inspirational single, "The Greatest Love of All" reminded us that the children are our future and to treat them well and let them lead the way.

In the 1960's, 70's, and 80's Black music was good, plain and simply good. It was soulful, funky, rhythmic and blue and good. Whether it got us through a painful break up, got us caught up in a new romance, got us in the mood, got us to the altar, or got us up off our feet and onto the dance floor, the music had a message of love, hope, and unity and entertained us all the while. The music was good right on up to the early nineties when Queen Latifah sung about U-N-I-T-Y and challenged any one disrespecting sisters with the question, "Who you calling a bitch?" Then, just like that the music changed. In what seemed like the blink of an eye Poof, things took a swift 180 and switched up.

Remember when we used to love and trust our men instead of being suspicious, wondering if they just wanted us for the bubbles in the back of our waistlines? It was easy to grant them with our hearts, undying love and utmost devotion because our dear brothers used to have our backs and would fight somebody to defend our honor if they stepped to us the wrong way. When L.L. Cool J cried that he needed love and would take his jacket off just so his sweetie pie could sashay her way on over a puddle, that's when we knew our men saw us as queens; something to be cherished, placed on a pedal stool and adored.

What they used to sing about used to make us feel good, but now we feel insulted. We used to feel uplifted, now we feel degraded. Our bodies used to be beautiful and sacred, to be had and shared with only that special someone, but now our bodies are gawked at, exploited, and used as mere sexual objects, simply to be disposed of and disregarded after ejaculation. Those sweet endearing lyrics of, "sugar pie honey bunch, you know that I love you", has vanished right along with the talented men who wrote and recited them. Not long ago bitch used to be baby, hoe used to be honey, and sex used to be making love. So what happened to the brother that used to sing his sweet song of love and devotion to his woman, not his bitch? Where is he?

By all accounts he's most likely somewhere stranded on the island of pop culture, hypnotized by the Black woman's booty and the way it sways to the rhythm of his lustful thoughts. Or he's on the Subway or the Metro bus, strolling the streets or moving through the malls of America snapping his fingers, bopping his head up and down, humming out the soundtrack to his life, which like so many of his fellow lost young brothers plays like hard-core acoustic porn, chock full of sexually perverted suggestions and misogynistic declarations. The raunchy music that's pumped into his ears through his headphones has become his native language, a strange and foreign dialect used to degrade and disrespect our women.

Listen to our sisters' souls come undone at the mouths of our brothers. After just one song, he unravels the many resilient and complex pieces it took years for Black women to construct. Black women have stood strong in the face of racism, and oppression, taken it with the stride only a sister could. As little girls we've cried when scary men dressed in white sheets came in the middle of the night, galloped off with our fathers, only to find the lifeless body of the first man we ever loved, the man who nurtured us, protected us, and provided for us, hanging from a tree with a noose tied around his neck the next morning.

As wives we've watched our strong husbands get whipped, humiliated, beat, shamed, skinned alive, stripped of their pride, violated, degraded, maimed and emasculated right in front of our tear filled eyes. Then after having to witness our men forced to surrender all their power leaving them unable to protect us, we were penetrated by pink penises and impregnated by foreign semen. We were forced to give birth to light skinned wavy haired babies whose sweet little faces, sprinkled with the same cinnamon freckles of the monsters who raped us, served as a constant reminder of our exodus out of our African homeland and pilgrimage into a cold distant land.

As mothers we've had our sons snatched from our wombs to get sold into slavery, mutilated for whistling at White women, sent to prison for crimes they did or did not commit and shot to death in south central Los Angeles, the south side of Chicago, New Orleans' ninth ward, Houston's 5th ward, Miami Dade county, or downtown Detroit.

After all of this we still didn't break down (or at least it appears as if we didn't), but here comes our brothers and for a recording contract equipped with a fat check and a spot on the pop charts they're willing to shred our self-esteem into tiny little pieces, slash our self-confidence with their tongues, and reduce our self-worth to mere ashes in public for all to hear (music) and for all to see (videos).

It doesn't matter if we graduated college magna cum laude, doesn't mean a thing that if we gave birth to and single-handedly reared many nations, and some of them could care less if we paid all the bills and cooked all the meals so that they could survive and be comfortable, making it easier for them to be where they are today. None of that matters when at the click of a button and the turn of the dial, we hear our "brothers" raping us with their words. Black women are being verbally assaulted by Black men and other Black women through the music a whole generation has written off as pure entertainment.

Then, as if that wasn't bad enough we have to sit back and watch some of our boys go to jail behind some make-believe mess they saw in a video or was inspired to do through the lyrics of a song. Like the snot nosed, wannabe cool, private school privileged kid who sneaks outside of his suburban, two-parent, two-car garage home to slang dope in the 'hood. The same 'hood his parents forbade him to step foot in because they knew firsthand how dangerous it could be. That's where they themselves were raised, but long since went to college, got a good job and fled the crime, the crack and the crips in exchange for a nice comfortable life in the 'burbs where they didn't have to worry about their kids getting involved in crime, crack or the crips.

When white bread kids like this get caught, and they almost always get caught because they're not real ganstas, what's the usual case? They were trying to be down by trying to live up to a false image of blackness, which in the mainstream media always equates to some stereotypical likeness of a thug, a crook, a hustler or a pimp. Sexual indiscretion, lack of self-control and disregard for laws, rules or authority is supposed to be the epitome of cool.

Those forces that be, in charge of what television and radio programs stream across the airwaves and what makes the final tracks on a CD understand the appetite of audiences for seeing and hearing ruthlessness and ignorance among minorities. They feed us, we eat it up. Money out of our pockets, money into their pockets to keep airing the ignorance. Acting like a nigger is profitable entertainment. And keeping it real most of it is just acting. Press the record button and watch how quick an average cool tempered Joe will be up in the camera or on the mike showing off, pretending to be hard, doing and saying things he wouldn't normally do or say if the camera or microphone wasn't there. In fact most of the craziness that makes the final cut on a movie, video or CD got there because it's outrageous, out of the ordinary.

The truth is a lot of rappers are squeaky clean kids from the suburbs and working class neighborhoods who are themselves trying to keep up with this thug-like image. The ones who are from the 'hood are either rapping about an experience one of their homeboys went through or rapping about the life they *used* to live. Drug dealing, hustling on street corners, gangbanging and all of the other delinquencies ghetto life entails had to be left behind in order to be successful in the music world. Rap skills and talent can only get a brother so far, he's got to be smart, business savvy, professional and for the most part law abiding. After all he's dealing with lawyers, accountants, label executives, image consultants, producers, directors, agents, the media and other professional people who've invested money and time into his career with a lot riding on his success.

In other words he can't be a dummy. Like a chest player he's got to be sharp, know the game, study his opponent and predict his opponents' next move, all while strategically planning his own next move. One misstep and his career could be finito. Surrounding himself with the wrong type of people, listening to bad advice, sleeping with the wrong women, getting into illegal or petty mischief with fools who aren't doing anything worthwhile with their own lives and would love to see him fall back down to their level, could end it all for him. So rappers, as loyal as they claim they are to their hoods, don't actually live in the hood because there's too much trouble in the hood. So like a Beverly Hillbilly who just struck oil, they chunk up the deuces to the hood the moment the first check is cashed from the record deal, moving to million dollar mansions in gated communities, exchanging roaches, welfare and repossessed cars for butlers, Bentleys and British stock options.

The truth is being a thug will either have you dying early of some painful horrible death like getting shot up on your own block with otherwise nosey people claiming not to have witnessed a thing because really, who wants to be a snitch? Or being a thug will end up having you face down, booty up on a cold concrete prison floor giving some big swole thick neck brother the ride of his life. Or worst still, you will have lived your whole life hustling, dealing, thieving, losing money chasing fast women, that by the time you're like 60-65 instead of preparing for retirement with a nice little nest egg to rest on in your golden years you'll be so strapped for cash that you'll end up flipping burgers, scrubbing toilets, washing windows, or unemployed altogether because with a criminal record, no legitimate work experience and an aging body what other options do you have?

Yet there are millions of little young dummies and old fools out here living out the lyrics to somebody's song because they misinterpreted the actual struggle for the shine of the struggle. The glorified edited version of the story that comes neatly wrapped in clear plastic and sells in the CD section at Best buy for $11.99 or an iTunes download could never tell the full story because the full story is too ugly. The hood is full of tired old bums who never made it out, filled to the brim with broken dreams and cups running over with rum and regret because they wasted their youth being cool, snorting their future up their noses, smoking the years away, screwing any and everything in a skirt.

Then there are the millions of little hot mommas running around dropping it and popping it, up in the mall trying to find the cute little strapless or backless top that chick had on in so-and-so's video. Young girls, six and seven years old know how to whine their waists and shake their skinny little booties precisely to the beat of any hip-hop song out on the radio. Looking at today's videos you can see where they get it from too. Light skinned chicks laced in the finest designer wears, sporting the flyest professionally done hair extensions and carrying most of their weight in their behinds are all up in the videos soaking up all the male attention. The eyes of our precious baby girls twirl around and around mesmerized by the lure of fame and the promise of potential riches as they fill up with images of these beautiful highly paid hip-hop whores.

Our girls are too young to understand that although video girls receive the attention and the shine of the limelight they are ultimately dogged, disrespected and dismissed the second the director yells cut. After all they're just the video girl, the decoration, the prop, used as an ornament to make the main attraction, the star rapper look good. After the show is over the big time rapper has his boys on set or backstage like, *what's up*. A few clueless vixens may turn their noses up in the air thinking they've made it to wobbling, wiggling and jiggling their derrières and other oversized body parts in hip-hop videos off of their dancing skills or sweet and charming personality or because they're on the high end of the intellectual hierarchy but most of these girls know what time it is. They know if they're not giving up the goodies or passing out the punani, or at least putting it out there on display, they're worthless and easily replaceable by another pretty face, slim waist and apple bottom.

We know that sex sells, duh, but show me something different. Sex in exchange for money is prostitution, but the hip-hop industry is doing a good job of convincing us that they're not prostituting these girls' minds, bodies and spirits although it's plain to see that they are. Baby girl may not be out strutting the street corner stepping over crack pipes or dirty needles alongside the zombie-like crack heads, but how else do you refer to a woman who shows off her cultured black pearls whenever she needs her rent paid, hair done or a new outfit to add to her already extensive and exclusive collection.

But the really clueless ones are the men who draw from this example when they go out searching for a new misses. The ones who bypass their wholesome hometown honeys and go straight for the bi-racial babes with big tits out to here, blonde weave down to there and bodacious booty bursting out of their jeans. The kind of chick who is identical to what he's shown in rap video after rap video after rap video. Or even worst when he expects the regular wife or girlfriend he already has to cater to his every need and want, fulfill every unconventional sexual fantasy stirred up in his head, or look a certain way based on an unattainable standard of beauty, which so happens to be the video girl look.

Where are we headed when there's an army of little girls, and young men coming up, who are absolutely devoted to dressing like, acting like, speaking like, and embodying the foolish caricatures on T.V.? Future doctors and lawyers, congressmen and congresswomen, small business owners and CEO's of fortune 500 companies who will someday be running the country, making laws and decisions that affect and influence our way of life, health and financial affairs are today up in somebody's club screwing a complete stranger in the dank dirty bathroom stall, while Lil' Wayne plays overhead. I'm scared just imagining where we'll be in 50 years.

Now HIV is burning down homes in the Black community, spreading like wildfire, taking lives first and asking questions last. Black women are catching it just as fast as they would catch the sniffles during flu season and Black men, especially those low down, down low brothers are passing it out just the same. All over the world Blacks are catching AIDS at a higher rate than any other group, but yet and still we pervert sex and manufacture that perversion through our music more proficiently than any other group.

B.E.T. tells us to Rap-it-up in their *safe sex, get tested, know your status* campaign, then they turn around and air all access videos with honey brown beauties unwrapping all of their clothes. The irony of it all is if you followed the lyrics to the songs that are playing in heavy rotation on some of our hottest hip-hop stations and on B.E.T. they would sure enough lead you to the free clinic itching or literally dying for a chance to not only wrap it up, but to lock it up until marriage.

All the AIDS education in the world is not going to stop the disease from multiplying if our entertainers don't take the initiative to stop glorifying multiple sex partners. Forget about pinning little red ribbons to our shirts, observances, memorials or marching up and down in a Save Our Life parade on AIDS day if we don't first hold our performers accountable every other day. So while B.E.T. is saying wrap it up, I'm pleading for us to clean it up first. Stop supporting and buying and downloading and bootlegging and please stop filling your ears with music that promotes a decaying lifestyle.

We've got to reach a point where we put our feet down and say enough is enough already, although the point should've been reached a long time ago. We've got to develop the ability to discern between self-destruction and entertainment. If the Bible says death and life are in the power of our tongues and our community is dying by way of HIV and AIDS, other diseases and violence, we've got to ask ourselves who among us has been conversing with death. Who's been inviting him into our homes, introducing him to our kids, making him a cup of coffee and sitting down at the table with him for a friendly chat? Could it be the rappers who poison our minds by way of music with their catchy tunes and hard to resist harmonies? Or is it the media outlets that air their music and nasty music videos, scarcely censored and barely filtered to reduce the icky-ness that we view? Or is the whole industry to blame?

The hip-hop industry is a multimillion dollar empire with tremendous power and authority over Black culture, Black people's attitudes and their standard of living. Hip-hop holds so much influence over the way young Black people live their lives that it should not only bare most of the brunt for their social disorder, but it should come up with and make moves towards a solution. For starters, up and coming rappers, who are the future of hip-hop, should present themselves respectfully as public figures instead of clowns. Image is everything and the way you dress and carry yourself says almost just as much about your level or seriousness and ability to be a big player in the rap game as anything you spit on the mike. Pull your pants up off of your thighs so that they can fit properly around your waist, spit out the gold grill and retire the word 'nigga' because it's old and you sound stupid.

Next, try creating descent music that elevates the spirit instead of degrading it. True, everybody doesn't have the wisdom to be a conscious rapper, but at least try to cleverly incorporate some important life lessons you've learned along the way into your rhymes. Every song doesn't have to be a club banger, paying homage to low budget strippers and their astonishing ability to work the pole. Appeal to our intellect, not just our carnal senses. From time to time make us actually use a brain cell or two by writing a complex rhyme with an original theme about a significant issue going on in the world. People will still listen. People will still buy. Even if they don't buy, the spiritual pay out for being conscious and clean is far greater than the fleeting riches attained by commercially selling out.

Last, get the smut out. In America, we (Black people) are the culture with the highest rates of HIV and AIDS, the highest rate of teenage pregnancy and children born out of wedlock, the highest rate of adults never to get married in the first place, the highest number of men imprisoned, the highest rate of poverty, and the highest number of people unemployed. What's even worst is the economic turmoil that has hit the country in recent years, has hit us over the head like a ton of bricks burying us in the rubble. If we were in it before, we're really in it now, not living, but surviving, barely, and mustering up the last bit of strength we have not to dig ourselves out of the ditch, but to just shovel the dirt out from in front of our faces just so we can get enough air to breathe.

We have a generation lost, feet stuck in the mud and an entire industry with the power to get them moving in a positive direction, but it's got to get the smut out. With all of the problems we face as a race, there should be a massive public uprising to clean up the music. It's filthy. Why sing songs paying tribute to alcoholic beverages when our kids aren't even making smart decisions sober? Why sing songs praising chicks who give good head when these little girls are already fast as it is and don't have their heads on straight? Why brag about cracking a nigga's skull open, and your past life as a drug dealer when a Black man who actually makes it across the stage to receive his highschool diploma, has a better chance of going off to jail than he does going off to college? What we're listening to now makes no sense and it needs to change.

However, there's too much money to be made in the industry off the backs of misguided young women with low or no self-esteem and young men with a fetish for drooling over their curvaceous bodies. Too much paper to be had preaching the gospel of drug deals, sex with no strings attached, violence and profanity. And unfortunately, just like a woman who's been told a good piece of gossip, money talks. So for now Rap continues to be rebellious, aggressive, bold, outspoken, commanding and unapologetically nonconformist music. What Rock was in the nineteen-seventies, and heavy metal in the eighties, rap is in the new millennium, only it's ten times as potent with no indication of fading out, simmering down, or cooling off on the horizon. This crunk-induced, rhythm and blues infused, soul inspired, heir to the throne of funk music is in fact about ready to boil on over and explode into a ferocious cross-cultural catastrophe.

Long since tip-toeing up the front lawns of suburban America, then jumping the gate into rural country town, U.S.A. where White boys in the corn fields of Nebraska have been tying bandanas around their heads and covering their blond locks with wave caps and do-rags, hip-hop has grown wings flying across oceans to be an international entity. From Brazil to Botswana teenagers who can't speak a lick of English can recite every word to a rap song and some of them, too poor to even afford a pair of shoes will still dance right along to the beat. Tell me who or what besides God almighty can silence ghetto America's creation, the same creation that from continent to continent has the force to rock the whole world, shake an entire generation down to its very core rushing in like a Biblical flood to control their clothes, shoes, speech, hairstyles, attitudes and sexual politics.

Remember the beginning? Africa, drums, rhythm, rhyme, poetry center stage with a backdrop of booming beats. Inequality, police brutality, broken down neighborhoods, but the feeling of reprieve because we had a musical outlet to talk about what's going on, why it's going on and how to change it. Remember us united singing sweet powerful songs with true and engaging lyrics that didn't lie, floss, front, degrade or slander another Brother's character. Rap has roots as real and as raw as the gritty neighborhoods where it originated and the power to keep on influencing generations to come.

Parents had better talk to their kids quick fast, because whether they like it or not Hip-hop is here to stay. With its feet up on their couches, warm and cozy it's the language most of their kids are speaking and relating to. Parents need to let them know the origin of the "N" word, how its original definition is rooted in racism and why it's not cool to say with an 'er or an 'a attached to the end, although rappers preach otherwise. Parents should explain what's going on in our culture; the trend of sex with no strings attached, the violence, the Godlessness, the materialism and provide them with the tools they'll need to guard themselves against such because it's too easy to get caught up. Parents should let them know why some women don't have respect for themselves and why some men take advantage of them and how it's sadly glamorized on T.V. or in the lyrics of their favorite songs. Parents, don't just hand them the remote control, cover your eyes, ears and mouth pretending all is well.

Things are different, this is not your parents or grandparent's generation. The hands-off approach may have worked in the fifties when teenagers hung out at the local malt shop, drank milkshakes, listened to doo-wop on the juke box then made it home by 8:00pm to watch Leave it to Beaver, but these are new and strange times. Teenagers are hauling fake ID's to get into the club, guzzling down Tequila shots, popping ecstasy and swapping STD's as casually as if they were trading autographed baseball cards. These are not the kinds of times for parents to be shy, uncomfortable or at a loss for words. The subject of sex, racism and violence especially in rap music has got to be approached aggressively head on and if not by the parents, trust and believe somebody else in the child's life will be schooling them.

To all my hip-hop heads I say, I truly respect your craft, but it's got to come under some heavy construction before it does more destruction, sinking Black people's morality further down into the immoral abyss it currently lays. The devil has a way of spinning his wicked wand around turning what was intended for good into iniquity and rap is no exception. For a little bit of cash, jewels, cars, women and fame many of these rappers have sold their souls to the devil and in exchange the devil is using them to spread his message of self-hate and self-destruction. The chilling messages many rap songs have not so discretely been sending is what corrupts the true sound and the beauty the music was intended to be.

Brothers, if you can make it through one of their songs without feeling sexually aroused or violent, if the music uplifts your spirit, makes you feel powerful and strong as a Black man then the added bonus is that it'll have a good beat. There are still really good rappers out there with something meaningful to say while using creative and inspiring ways to say it over the pound of a nice rhythm. You might have to search a little harder, likening your pursuit to finding needle in a haystack, but they do really exist. Just remember kids are tuning their parents out and guess what they're tuning into, your music. You've got our young peoples ears so take advantage of the opportunity and use your voice to say something significant.

Homosexuality:
How it's destroying our Community

Some sisters say they can sense it. Even when a brother lifts his right hand in the air and places his left hand on a ten foot stack of Bibles swearing before God that he's not, these all knowing sisters say they recognize. He doesn't have to switch his hips from side to side when he walks as if he's got something permanently wedged between his legs. His voice doesn't have to be that high pitch falsetto talking that *uh-huh, honey-child, girl please* sister type vernacular. Brother man doesn't even have to be a licensed beautician obsessed with hair and make-up, or fixated on fashion; polished Stacy Adams, Cartier belt buckles, cashmere Burberry half coats or pre-occupied with decorating, window drapes, matching bedspreads and comforters. Yet and still from a mile away these intuitive women guarantee they can spot a gay, bi-sexual, or down low brother out of a crowd.

But me, see I'm not one of those women. Take a fine, sweat drenched, muscles ripping out of his jersey, basketball playing brother and to me there are no signs. If he's not flamboyantly prancing around in pink stilettos acting all feminine looking like Liberace and RuPaul's little brother, but on the other hand is rugged, hard core, brute and masculine then there's no way I can possibly differentiate him from any straight man walking down the street.

Today the homosexual brother is the brother with the cool swagger, the white-T, baggy jeans and the cap to the side sporting dreads, braids or a fade underneath. He's that fine, slim brother on the B-ball court stealing the heart of every girl on the side line while he massacres all the other brothers with his mean jump shot. He's that built brother at the gym perfecting an already perfect set of abs, using weights and barbells like tools of artistic design to add even more finely chiseled cuts to his beautifully sculpted body.

Today's homosexual brother is the faithful member of thousands of America's churches. He might be the Sunday school teacher, the usher, church deacon, choir director, youth pastor or more times than we care to admit he might even be the head pastor. One thing he is not is typical, average or easily identifiable as a gay man, or at least not to me. Because I can't point him out of a crowd and say, "Look, there he is, that's him he's gay," I'm constantly watching my back, looking over my shoulder, forever suspicious and paranoid not knowing who is what these days.

Especially since there's an emerging culture of Black men who have sex with other men, but do not consider themselves gay, lying, misrepresenting themselves, disguising the facts, abandoning reality, replacing the truth for half truths, going through life faking and fronting. These courage deprived men are selfishly tip-toeing behind their women's back, slipping under each other's sheets and without thought, conscious or remorse are just as easily slipping back into their marriages and relationships. Catching HIV or any of those other life threatening STD's are shoved to the back of their minds where common sense, sense of morality and sense of decency have been conveniently stored away too. Lust clouds their better judgment and confusion leaves them indecisively bouncing back and forth between men and women on any given mood.

Books, movies and magazines refer to them as men on the down-low, but away with the cute, cushiony, non-offensive terms, I just call them low-down men. A man who decides to get it on with another man unbeknownst to his wife or girlfriend, a man who doesn't mind playing Russian roulette with his health, squandering his integrity, shaming his family or possibly risking his career for a quick romp in a cheap motel, now that's the lowest of the low. Corrupt politicians are finding themselves mixed up in sleazy bathroom sex scandals, seemingly decent family men are getting caught in the back seat of their minivans with their pants down around their ankles and young boys are being lured by online predators, molested by clergymen, little league coaches, gym teachers and their mothers live-in boyfriends.

Brothers are flipping out on all levels and it's sad, but their women and children, ignorant to what they're doing on the down low, are the ones to feel sorry for. Because when the lights get switched on, when stuff starts hitting the fan, when the HIV test comes back positive, when homeboy is eventually dragged out of the closet, albeit kicking and screaming, but dragged nonetheless, the misses and the kiddies are the ones unfairly sentenced to a lifetime of sorting through all the skeletons Mr. Low-down has been hiding in that closet.

Low-down brothers add insult to injury on a community that's already broken and suffering from the wounds of racism, poverty, and discrimination. Wounds we've yet to fully recover from, wounds we haven't even scratched the surface on, wounds we've neglected to treat, medicate, let alone heal. But what Black women are trembling at the knees over, the thought that their man might be creeping with another man, is just a symptom of a greater sickness. The greater sickness being homosexuality.

Whether he's miserably married to a woman and sexing a man on the side to release some tension from an unhappy situation at home, or whether he's gay all the way, out in the open, out there having fun, singling and mingling, the fact still remains that the Black family is bruised and battered from any and all types of homosexual activity. The turmoil these low-down, down-low brothers have caused can't even hold a candle to the greater destructive force that fuels their transgressions, the demonic spirit of homosexuality.

Our brothers are literally being dragged into the pits of hell by the spirit of sodomy, blindly walking into a life full of pain, misery, disorder, depression and disease. There is no peace in their path, no rest, no joy, just a constant struggle with their emotions, a never ending battle against suicidal thoughts, emptiness and confusion. But the really messed up part about it is, we as a community have been more than willing to sit back and watch them stagger down this dead end road, even patting some of them on the back telling them, 'it's good that they've found themselves a boyfriend'.

Wealthy Black families have even been duped into spending thousands of dollars to send their sons to lie on a psychologist couch so some doctor can explain away why they've been lusting after other boys. Parents paying top dollar so their sons can learn to recite daily positive self-affirmations to keep them from blowing their brains out and to teach them that their perverted thoughts are normal. Thinking a few sessions of counseling can rub away the stigma attached to being gay and diminish any doubts that what he's doing and feeling is wrong so the boy can feel like his sexual urges and affections towards other boys are healthy and simply a part of his natural development as a male.

'I've graduated from this prestigious top notch ivy-league university with 18 million advanced degrees so I know-it-all.' psychologist are persuading our young men to come to terms with their homosexual orientation, embrace it, accept it, hold their heads up high and proudly strut on out of the closet when on the contrary, The Word of God encourages homosexuals to instead clean out the closet by getting down on their knees, accepting the Lord's forgiveness and getting right. Save the money and the time because no matter how many college degrees decorate their office wall, no psychologist in the world is going to be able to patch together the pieces of a broken life shattered by perverted homosexual acts, thoughts and lifestyles if it hasn't first been brought to Christ.

Yet, like lost little sheep every day more and more of our young men and young women are being led astray. They're being told that as sexual beings it's alright to experiment with their sexuality by playing sexual games with each other in the bathroom, fondling one another at sleepovers or on the play ground. There are actually supposedly responsible adults here in America; teachers, psychologist, and doctors who'll write sexual play among boys off as natural, normal, healthy even and simply a part of growing up.

Never mind that every day another brother puts a gun to his temple and shoots a hole straight through his head because hey, it's not natural, normal, or healthy. A mans sexuality and sexual orientation can't be taken lightly, abused, fiddled with, tampered or misused in any kind of way without it taking a toll on his mind, soul and spirit. Men jumping head first outside the bounds of nature is wrong and damaging to the very essence of who they are as men.

Of the many parts a man is made of, the biggest chunk of who he is is tied to his sexuality and gender. Before he's anything in this world, he is first a man. Before he is Black, he is a man. Before he is White, he is a man. Before he ever picks up a brick to lay down a foundation on this earth for himself and for his family he is a man, made in God's own image. Adam never knew his own ethnicity, never knew his race, never knew whether he was black, white, yellow, brown, or red, all he knew was that he was a man and as a man, he had a job to do, to look after the earth and its creatures. The good book leaves us to only guess what shade his skin was painted or what language he spoke, but his gender and subsequently his role on earth as a man is unmistakably defined: guardian over God's creation, protector and provider.

If a man "marries" another man, which one of them is the protector? Who does God appoint to be the provider? I'm confused just thinking about it and I'm sure those entangled in same sex relationships are left scratching their heads as well, making up the rules of their bizarre union as they go. While the Word of God says wives are to submit themselves to their husbands and husbands are to love their wives as Christ loved the church (Colossians 3:18), the Bible makes no reference to wives submitting themselves to their wives and is silent on how husbands are to love their husbands. Homosexuals have taken it upon themselves to rewrite the Bible and write their own gospels, *the gospel according to themselves,* as the Bible, no longer reigning supreme as the spiritual authority in their lives collects dust on their bookshelves.

While I'm a firm believer that what two consenting grown folks do behind closed doors is their own business, none of mines, yours or anybody's, homosexuality up and jumped out of the bedroom into the schools, the court rooms and the church. Gone are the days where people kept their sinning on the hush, quiet and on the low. When people just did what they did and didn't tell anybody because it just wasn't cool to have your business out there in the streets. Now they're out and about wearing rainbow colored wrist bands and waving their rainbow colored flags, marching, parading around, saying it loud, "I'm gay and I'm proud".

And don't criticize their lifestyle either, oh no, don't say anything that might even slightly hint to homosexual behavior being strange, unnatural, weird or immoral. Opposition is met with swift and brutal consequences, accusations of homophobia, accusations of intolerance and accusations of hate speech. Even the Church is being attacked for speaking out against homosexuality. Since churches are exempt from paying taxes there are some nutty people out here who are pushing hard to get legislation passed that would cause churches to lose their tax exemption status if they preach anti-homosexual doctrine in their pulpits.

Taking it a step further, some wacky homosexual groups are even lobbying congress to create a bill that would make speaking out against homosexuality a hate crime, a hard core felony punishable by up to five years in jail. Under their proposed law, church leaders could be criminally prosecuted for quoting Bible scriptures like Leviticus 20:13, claiming the thousand year old sacred text which through reading, and studying, and applying its principals to their everyday lives, have brought peace and comfort to millions of people around the world. But they would make it seem like quoting scripture would now somehow incite violence against poor little helpless homosexuals who need legal protection against the hatemongering Christians.

Last time I checked the Constitution hadn't been amended or rewritten. Free speech is still free meaning, as Americans, we have the right to say what we want, when we want, how we want regardless of who it offends. From all reports America is still a free country, but I guess that only means free for homosexuals and liberals. They want the freedom and the right to do as they please, say as they please, and live as they please without criticism, but we, those who oppose homosexuality, are automatically shut down and told to shut up when we speak out against it.

And as far as gay Black men are concerned, if the church won't budge and somehow rewrite scripture to accommodate their beliefs and lifestyles, then some brothers are leaving the church. The same church in which most of them were raised, protected in and supported by all their lives. Suddenly the long held traditions of the church and Christianity are irrelevant to their lives, outdated and unsuitable because they have a sexual urge that isn't cohesive with Biblical teachings.

Then on the flip side, there are the brothers who simply hide within the church and blend in with the rest of the congregation on Sunday morning while living their double lives Monday through Saturday. No, they will not leave the church. They love the church, serve in the church, are heavily involved in several church ministries and would not dare think to withdraw themselves from the flock, but they also have sexual urges that are incompatible with Biblical teachings. Confessing their sins to *He who is faithful and just* to forgive them of their sins, and reaching out for real redemption from the Lord along with fasting and intercessory prayer from the church would mean having to break off their lusty male on male relationships, a decision for one reason or the other some of them can't come to, or through sheer disobedience to God, many of them refuse to carry out.

Sincere sympathy to the brothers who know in their hearts that while God condemns homosexuality, he still loves them, Jesus still died for them, can forgive them of all their sins (homosexuality included) and has the power to heal them of their sick thoughts and perverse desires. But those brothers struggle everyday with homosexual cravings, they fight every day to resist the pull, but more times than they care to admit they fall into temptation. Despite the thumbs up approval signal they're given by an increasingly gay friendly society, a lot of men truly don't want to be gay because deep down inside they know it's wrong, but the devil is a beguiling little sucker.

By nature we are all sinners and the flesh is weak, in our own power we don't have the strength to fight against the temptations of satan. Using willpower to overpower sexual temptation, homosexuality included is like showing up to a gunfight with a butter knife. No brainer, you lose. Which is why some brothers could've gone years without the urge. They could've buried all those homosexual feelings by marrying a woman, having children and joining a church, but just when their life seems like it's all intact, just when they think they've conquered those homosexual yearnings, satan will sneak up from behind, tap them on the shoulder and with the slightest gesture it's all over. A tight hug from an old college buddy that may last just a tad too long, a firm handshake from an attractive colleague after the close of a business deal, a glimpse of a sexy movie star without his shirt on, on a magazine cover, something small can trigger those old feelings, reigniting passions within himself that he'd long since thought had cooled.

Like recovering drug addicts trying to stay clean, they're struggling not to think about "gettin' wit" a dude because they know once they've lost the battle in their minds, they've lost the battle period because homosexuality is a spirit. The struggle against it is powerful and real. The Bible says, *"We wrestle not against flesh and blood, but against principalities, against powers, against the rulers of the darkness of this world, against spiritual wickedness…"* (Ephesians 6:12). Some brothers just can't kick the craving because there's a demonic spirit hard at work waging war against them.

But homosexuality shouldn't be singled out among other sins because there are spirits waging war against all of us, preying on our weaknesses and innermost forbidden desires. Alcoholism is a spirit, depression is a spirit, pedophilia is a spirit, gambling is a spirit, and many other mental and emotional afflictions are spirits. We all struggle against something. Some of us struggle with fornication, some of us struggle with lying, envying others or stealing office supplies from work, for others it's a struggle to manage money, abusing credit and staying out of debt is a day to day battle, but the thing that differentiates homosexuality is advocates of that lifestyle spend all their time, money and energy trying to convince us that there's nothing immoral about it. The family of an alcoholic will persuade him to check into rehab, chronic depression is treated with counseling and medication, a pedophile is thrown in jail, we seek forgiveness and repair of broken marriages for committing adultery through marriage counseling, but in the 21st century homosexuality is celebrated.

Two men intertwined in the confusion masquerading itself as love shouldn't be a celebrated sight. Instead of being celebrated for a lifestyle that may ultimately cause their untimely death through suicide or disease, these brothers need help, counseling, reparative therapy, and prayer, not approval and applause. They need our unconditional love, support and encouragement so that they are inspired to change. But most of all, more important than anything else, they need repentance and salvation. Only Christ has the power to break the chains Satan uses to bind our men to vile and disgusting thoughts which lead to vile and disgusting behavior. Behavior that despite their own efforts to stop, despite years of wrestling against those feelings, drowning themselves in bottles of Jack Daniels, conquering countless nameless, faceless women to prove their manhood and rid themselves of the homosexual syndrome, despite every desperate attempt they can't shake themselves loose.

If the Bible says, *we wrestle not against flesh and blood, but against spirits*, then the battle can only be won by a spirit, the Holy Spirit. All of these struggles require the holy spirit of God working inside of us to escape the temptation, because we can only live on the straight (pun intended) and narrow through His power, not our power.

However, some brothers refuse to repent and seek salvation, loving lust more than they love the Lord, figuring it's easier to hide their sins than to confront their sins and live differently. So they become choir directors, ministers of music, youth pastors or hold other important positions in the church. As long as nobody finds them out they're comfortable being suit and tie wearing, 'Jesus Loves Me' singing, Holy Ghost catching members of the congregation, blending in and not looking, acting, or appearing to be any different than the straight brothers. And when cornered with the question why they aren't married, or have girlfriends, or aren't courting any women from the church they lie and say they're too busy serving the Lord. Or worst, tired of the questioning they go out and find themselves a wife or girlfriend, maybe even have a few kids so people will stop their suspicious interrogations and their gossiping. Church folks can be oh so nosey. Yeah, I said it.

God's alter is open for confession and forgiveness, but many will not seek it because they are too entrenched in the lifestyle. They have too many people around them misquoting, mishandling and manipulating scripture so they come to believe that they don't have to change their behavior to be in line with what God says is right, because God somehow will change what He says is right. Sorry to bust somebody's bubble, but God doesn't change. He is the same yesterday, today, and forever and still the same after that. His Word can't be customized or tailored to better fit our needs, wants, or desires, no matter how overpowering our emotions may be. As much as people try to compromise God's words, stretch it out a little over here, chop it up a bit over there, leave this part out, or add that part in, from Genesis to Revelation homosexuality was, is and will remain for all eternity a sin.

With people trying to redefine God's word, it's no surprise they'd try to come up in here and redefine the family too. Homosexuals desperately want the legal right to get married so that they can legitimize their illegitimacy and call themselves a family. Gay couples, who obviously can't produce children on their own, flood adoption agencies with their checkbooks in tow in order to purchase third world orphans from overseas so they can call themselves a family. Lesbians, who obviously can't produce children on their own, flee to artificial insemination clinics to have their eggs implanted with intelligent, good-looking, high IQ super sperm so that with a little science mingled with technology, they too can call themselves a family. A mixed-up mangled mess of children with two daddies, and no mommy or two mommies, and no daddy: confusion on top of confusion disguising itself as a family.

Then to top it all off, seventy percent of all Black children born this decade will be born into single parent homes meaning close to 3 out of 4 of our most precious resources, our children, will come limping into the world through illegitimate relationships. Relationships where many of their parents never made true, loving commitments to one another. Relationships where they were unable to work out a proper plan for their own partnership, leaving them unable to properly partner in parenting.

Relationships where their parents played house by living together, paid bills together, slept in the same bed together, had kids together, did everything that married couples do, pretending to be married, but somehow couldn't bring themselves to actually jump the broom. Teaching their kids by example that marriage is not important, desirable, or valuable and that a marriage certificate is just a measly piece of paper.

Relationships where their parents don't live together so the child will have to pack an overnight bag and commute back and forth from one household to the next every other weekend, never having real stability or a sense of security. Where, since the child will spend a majority of their time at one household, and lesser time at the other household, the relationship with the part-time parent, usually the dad will never fully developed like it should if his presence were in the home full-time.

Single parents who are financially insecure and dependent upon the government to feed their children because they can't, single parents who are emotionally ill-equipped to take care of their children and so they don't and single parents who are children themselves; young, reckless, inexperienced, irresponsible, immature, and uneducated is the sad new definition of the Black family.

Black people are next in line to be added to the endangered species list because the Black family is quickly fading out of existence. We simply cannot survive, let alone thrive and prosper, or face any of the challenges of the future without the Black family intact. We can forget about higher educational achievements for our kids, eliminating poverty, reducing crime, lowering HIV rates, increasing job opportunities, or restoring a sense of pride within ourselves and respect for ourselves and each other if we can't preserve the most basic foundation of our community, the family. If we can't get our individual households in order, how are we to get the community in order?

This decade thousands of single Black women will reach the age of thirty and face the reality that they only have a lower chance of ever being married than Latina, Asian, or White women who'll have very few problems attaining husbands by the time they blown the candles out on their thirtieth birthday cake and beyond. In part due to an all out assault by gay Black men who deprive beautiful sisters of suitable men to marry while they're off fighting the government for a chance to marry each other. We already know we have to compete against White women for a Black man's attention, but now we have to compete against other men.

Let these silly people out here have their gay rights parades, their petitions and protests, their civil unions, commitment ceremonies and legislations to legalize gay marriages, along with their twisted definitions of family. Leave them alone, let them self destruct, let their own communities crumble and come undone by the wicked works of their own doing. As for us, Black women, we don't have to defend or agree with or be tolerant of this homosexuality business. 'Politically incorrect', 'homophobic', 'close-minded', 'narrow-minded', 'small-minded', we shouldn't give a flying flip what they call us because we, Black women, are the ones left alone without a decent pool of available men to marry and we're the ones infected with HIV from these brothers on the down low.

This isn't about stomping on the Constitution or blocking anyone from enjoying their free rights, and this isn't about force feeding our religious beliefs down anyone's throat, this is about survival; survival of the Black community and the very real fear of the extinction of the Black family. Black women shouldn't be approving, or supporting homosexuality, or made to feel guilty for not approving, or not supporting a social and moral sin with such harmful effects on our community and on us.

They're hurting us and they're hurting themselves. The number of gay Black men running around sexing every Tyrone, Deshawn, and Hakeem without a care in the world, a condom, or the thought that they could be carrying AIDS is absolutely mind blowing. Go to any gay bar or club in any major city around the country and you wouldn't believe it. AIDS is everywhere, like it's airborne or something. In the bathroom, behind the bar, in V.I.P., somebody's infected with something.

Pick any weekend out of the month and suppose an AIDS organization gave voluntary HIV testing to Black men entering popular gay night clubs. Anybody with a heart would gasp at the results. Statistically speaking, if such a study was done at any gay club in America frequented by Black men, the results would show approximately 28% percent or about one out of every four brothers from this study coming up positive. ONE OUT OF FOUR. That's a bone chilling, heart thumping, spine tingling, frightening quarter. A humungous number of seemingly random, nameless, faceless figures. But these numbers aren't just random, nameless, faceless figures; they equate into real life personalized tragedies. Each number has a name, each name has a face, and each face looks like that of our own sons, brothers, fathers, and friends, men we love and care about who are suffering and wasting away over a preventable sexual disease.

> *"...in the same way, their males also abandoned their natural sexual function toward females and burned with lust toward one another. Males committed indecent acts with males, and received within themselves the appropriate penalty for their perversion."*

> **-Romans 1:27, <u>International Standard Version</u>**

The public so often hears about the romantic aspect of gay relationships; how they love their boo, how they're so in love and just want to be viewed as normal, how they just want to be married and how they just want the same rights as all other Americans, but how many times do you hear about the dark side? Some downright nasty things can happen to the body during and after homosexual sex, stuff that you won't hear gay activist speak out on at their rallies and speeches, or when they appear on talk shows to defend their lifestyle. Incontinence, Hemorrhoids, rectal tearing, rectal fissures, anal cancer, anal warts and genital warts just to name a few.

Of course heterosexual sex poses health risks too, but almost all of these risks are averted once a couple has tested negative for STD's and there on out established monogamy, but for a homosexual, even safely wrapped inside a committed partnership the bed can be like a battle zone, dangerous and all too many times deadly. Reason being, the body is simply not designed for homosexual sex. The tissue around the anus is weak and can easily rupture, and due to contact with fecal matter (poop), which carries millions of microorganisms (germs), it's susceptible to all kinds of infections.

Now the anus is but a tiny hole no bigger than the size of a quarter with barely any flexibility. The little elasticity it does have is there for waste to easily extract out of it, but it's not stretching for anything to be inserted into it. To break it down, when a man tries to shove his penis into a recipient's anus the penis places pressure on the anus. The sphincter muscle (the circular muscle surrounding the anus) automatically shrinks and tightens to an even smaller size as if the body was saying, "No baby, ain't nothing getting up in here. I'm not designed for that." It's an involuntary reflex. The human eye has this same kind of reaction. Whenever something comes too close to our eyes we automatically flinch them shut to protect them. It's not a conscious thing, we're not cognizant of it, we just do it innately because it's the Lord's perfect design to keep our eyes healthy and safe.

The anus can't even get wet on its own. There are no glands down there for moisture to dispense out of; the brain doesn't trigger any hormones for it to lubricate when a person becomes sexually aroused or anything. Common sense would tell us that if this part of the body doesn't become moist for insertion nothing was meant to be inserted into it, but common sense seems to be a dead and dying notion these days. To our folly humans always try to manipulate nature and with homosexual sex, not all homosexual sex, but in general with homosexual sex a few hours of fun means major manipulation of the body on multiple levels. Creams have to be rubbed here, oils and ointments have to be spread there, tools have to be used, and toys are exploited just to make this part fit here, and that part squeeze into there. It's all just a mess. Even with a condom, condoms have a higher chance of breaking during anal sex than during vaginal sex because again, the rectum does not lubricate naturally.

Squirm uncomfortably in your seat or be embarrassed by what you're reading if you want, but this is real. This is what can happen to the precious bodies of our boys during homosexual intercourse. This is what a morally decomposing sick society promotes and passes off as innocent and harmless. This is what they want us to applaud and be tolerant of. I'm sorry, but I'm not going to give a standing ovation to the high rates of STD infections among my gay Black brothers; the HIV, the HPV, the Chlamydia, E.Coli infections, herpes, hepatitis, pubic lice, gonorrhea, typhoid fever and all the other diseases associated with the infectious nature of fecal matter or sexual intercourse in general.

This is not to scare anybody, but then again, it is. We ought to be scared, scared enough to speak up and speak out against this destructive way of life because far too many people are uneducated about the harmful effects of homosexual relations. They want us purposely uneducated. They want us to be sheeple, a mindless conformist society who they can pull the wool over our eyes so that they can slowly move in with their agenda without resistance. Oh yeah, homosexuals have an agenda, and they've gotten strong and aggressive with it. They want us rewrite ancient scripture or toss out our Bibles altogether, get rid of our beliefs, get with the times, validate their behavior, embrace their lifestyle, be accepting and be open-minded. Well, it's okay to be closed-minded sometimes. We need to close ourselves off to things that will destroy our community.

Homosexuality is a sin just like all other sins and according to the Bible, sin is sin is sin. Not providing for the children you fathered or gave birth to is a sin. Chemically altering your mind or numbing your emotions with drugs or alcohol is a sin. Promoting illicit sex, drug use and violence through the lyrics of a song is a sin. Self hatred and refusing to love women with skin the same tone as your own is not only a shame, but it too is a sin. Little white lie or big time deception, cheating on an exam at school or cheating on your wife, slipping a piece of candy from the corner store into your pocket without paying or robbing the corner store by gun point is all the same in the eyes of the creator. Sin.

All sins should be treated the same, that is, they all need to be brought to the cross of Christ, confessed and through faith in the Grace of God forgiven, but all sins are not the same. The ramifications for certain sins weight heavier on the soul and on the body than others. Two men sleeping together and creeping together trying to imitate what only a man and a woman can do, make love, is called out from among all the other sins and identified as an abomination. Shameful. Disgraceful. Dishonorable. Displeasing to the Lord.

God gazes down on his creation with a fractured heart grieving the loss of every single Black man who's life could've been written like the script of an epic story; could've met and fell in love with a beautiful woman, could've been a faithful husband and loving father to their children, could've been a role model to the generation of young Black men coming up without role models, guidance or proper examples on how to be men.

If our gay brothers use their God given gift of manhood to its fullest potential they could have the greatest testimony; the ability to be leaders of the community, protectors of the community, and providers of the community. They'd have the power to be at the forefront of the movement that leads Black people out of darkness, disadvantage and despair towards a future where more of our sons have Dr. at the beginning of their names and more of our daughters have M.D. at the end of theirs. A future where more of our boys aspire to run corporations instead of running from the cops, and where our girls dream of becoming self-made millionaires instead of just having a baby by one. A future where two parent families are the norm and single parent families are the exception to the rule, not the rule.

This could be the legacy brothers leave on this earth if they follow in the footsteps of Christ, building the foundation that strengthens the Black community, creating a smoother path for future generations to walk through. This is the end story of Black men whose lives are spent submitting to God's will instead of submitting to their own desires, being obedient to His Word instead of being politically correct, guided by the Holy Spirit instead of led by the spirit of lust.

Unfortunately, instead of allowing the Lord to be the author, many men chose to scribble all over the pages of their life story, making a mess of it. Like kindergarteners who can't stay in the lines of their coloring books, homosexual men go outside the lines of God's will encountering heartache at every wrong turn and collecting a handful of sorrows along the way. Sexually transmitted diseases, depression, confusion, loneliness, death, the list goes on. Any time we consciously or unconsciously choose to step outside the boundary of God's plan for our life we choose to step outside of his protection and are left to wallow in the mess or our own making. Turning our back on the Creator never produced a pot at the end of the rainbow, happiness or peace, just misfortune and suffering.

The sad reality is most of our Black men will not leave the gay lifestyle because most of the people around them are giving them high-fives and congratulating them for living out in the open. On the contrary, some of the others are fire and brimstone preaching, holier-than-thou, self-righteous religious radicals so caught up in condemning them to hell to the point where the message of Christ's love and salvation gets completely blurred by indignant, arrogant and downright hateful rhetoric. We should in no way condone the gay lifestyle, but neither should we cast stones.

What we need to do is softly speak the truth in love, and we can love them while still standing firm in our principles. In fact, at a time when they're confused, lonely, and sexually assaulted daily by the devil, they need our love more than anything. The rest of the world is either telling them things to make them feel good, or telling them things to make them feel bad. The world is either tap-dancing around the truth making sure not to hurt homosexuals' feelings or crushing their already bruised and battered self-esteem.

Black men will repent and leave the lifestyle when Christ calls them from a life he declares is not for them and when they heed the calling. In the meantime, what we as a community need to be telling them are things that will save their lives and ultimately save their souls in the process. That is, we love you, God loves you, we will be there for you, God is there for you, but honey, God disapproves of your lifestyle choices, therefore so do we.

Thank you, Hallelujah:
A celebration of our men

Thank you. I know we don't say it often, it's just two simple words, but they've been a long time coming and a long time in the making. With all of the negative stereotypes plaguing Black men, from outside sources and sadly the ones that are self-inflicted, sisters sometimes forget to celebrate all the wonderful aspects of our men and in that neglectful state we might also nonchalantly pass over your contributions and accomplishments as if they're worth nothing, when in reality the hard work, the fortitude and sweat off your back is surely recognized and appreciated. For all the anger we sometimes hold inside our hearts and the resentment we carry in our souls towards you brother, we feel that much more love and appreciation. So with arms wide open full of forgiveness and with a heart jam-packed with firm faith in the belief that despite all the drama, the conflict, the hurt and pain, our miss-understandings, miss-communication and all the tears shed on your behalf, praising you is just and well deserved.

Thank you to all the wonderful Black men who we don't have to question, *why are brothers disappearing?* because we can look to our left or to our right and see you right by our side, your shoulders gently brushing up against our shoulders, holding our hands and ready to fight whatever battles life hurls at us, together.

A thousand sweet kisses to those fierce brothers, those Black warriors possessed with the spirits of their African ancestors who have stepped up in front of us leading us to a better tomorrow, unafraid and unwavering in their commitment to secure for their women, children and community, safety, security and stability by any and every means necessary.

Gracious thanks to all the Men, and by Men I mean men in every sense of the word, the Men who in spite of the emotional turmoil us women have put you through, in spite of our *I don't need you* declarations, spicy attitudes and sour moods which sometimes accompanies our independence, we can still glance behind us to see you supporting us in all our endeavors. Feels good to have someone back there pushing us forward, giving us that extra nudge to move us along when we get discouraged, fed up and feel like throwing in the towel. Thanks for having our backs.

There's nothing better than the slow exhale and the sigh of relief we take when the storms of life rush in with a fearful force catching us off guard, with its fiercely cold winds which causes us to lose all strength, buckle at the knees and drop to the ground, when the storm waters rush in sweeping us off of our feet we fight to swim upstream, but our arms grow weary and tired and so we're drowning and just to stay alive we hold our breath, but suddenly right before we cry what might surely be our last plea to God there's light, breath, energy and the soul soothing comfort of our brothers warm embrace. You may not have all the resources to rescue us, but just knowing that you are there for us with a sound mind, body and spirit is very necessary to our physical, spiritual and emotion well being. Cradled in your love and support we're able to weather the storm. Thank you.

Thank you for giving us just as much respect as you demand in the wake of an era where too many Black men have replaced the love and respect they once had for their women with the mistreatment, abuse and utter disrespect now common in our community. It is so good to know we're still viewed as Queens in some of our men's eyes, recognized and placed above other women in their lives because of the rich and royal heritage we share, the divine blood traveling through our veins. Our African ancestry taught us to value one another and hold each other in the highest regard so thank you graceful Kings for carrying on the teachings of our forefathers.

Thank you for being strong, intelligent, humble, hardworking and Godly when other brothers have allowed themselves to be a fulfillment of the stereotypes; spiritually weak, lazy, foolish, thoughtless, boastful and proud. Thank you for knowing who you are and not just standing up for what you believe in, but standing firm on those beliefs no matter how harsh the consequences. I love you, intelligent Black man who moves with conviction and refuses to sit still when there is an injustice in the world. You're so sexy when you get heated over a topic in the news that you feel passionate about, able to intellectually debate your position, backing it up with previous knowledge and real references instead of just saying *I don't like or agree with what's going on because I just don't.*

My heart belongs to the brother who knows that just because he graduated from some accredited university doesn't make him smart, but what makes him smart is his ability to exercise common sense, critical thinking, along with good judgment and who understands it's a must to challenge what "they" say instead of sitting back passively and comfortably nodding his head like a soft well trained puppy. I'm totally in love with the brother who realizes he doesn't have to blend in or tone down his "Blackness" in order to achieve success, neither does he have to sell-out, or compromise his values, he just has to work hard, pray even harder, continually walk in God's will and prosperity is guaranteed.

I'm absolutely impressed with Black men who are willing to try something new instead of shunning away from or making fun of the things they don't understand or aren't familiar with. Awestruck by Men who thirst for world knowledge, hunger for new experiences and crave wisdom knowing that the world is more than just what goes on in his own neighborhood or what meets the eye. Enthralled by men who don't take the easy way out by lying, hiding, ducking, ditching, dodging, or dulling his emotions with drugs and alcohol because he knows that trials and tribulations are pertinent to his growth as a human being and struggle is just a part of life he has to deal with. The more he knows, the more he grows so for him ignorance is not bliss, but knowledge is power.

I'm absolutely impressed with Black men who aren't ashamed to display their intellectual side by reading something other than the sports section or XXL magazine. Real brothers whose purpose in life doesn't consist of how many skirts they can get under or how much weed and alcohol they can consume, but their sense of fulfillment and pursuit of happiness comes from engaging themselves in activities to stimulate their minds, which are sharper than freshly filed blades, constantly expanding, creating and exploring all of its possibilities.

These brothers understand the prospects of what an education can allow them to achieve. They get how empowering a Black man with an education is to a society who automatically assumes he's ignorant and unlearned and they are forever working towards increasing knowledge because the educated Black man is mature enough to know that the attainment of knowledge is power, the nurturing of a thought is essential and its execution takes strength. Being smart and showing off their intelligence is not acting white, it's not un-cool or nerdy and it's definitely not being weak as some have been mislead to believe.

A man who diligently seeks to enrich his life and reach his highest potential through a personal relationship with the creator is like a finely cut Black diamond that's been chiseled to almost perfection. Rare, valuable and to be treasured. He's beyond the expensive tailored suits, the beautifully sculpted muscular body, the charm, the wit, the nice car he may drive or even the amount of women he can get. Strip away all of that from your average brother and your average brother is left bare, cold, naked, shivering and empty.

The money loving, paper chasing, workaholic brother who neglects his family because he feels nothing is more important than his career or the lazy, refuses-to-get-a-job-even-if-his-kids-go-hungry brother or even the self professed player who believes the measure of his masculinity is defined by how many weak minded women he can talk into bed, well all of these men are reduced to nothing in the presence of a Godly man.

A spiritually minded man, that is a man with the wisdom to know he's made in God's own image and as an earthly representation of the divine works hard, provides for his family, cherishes his woman, and respects himself and those around him, a man like this is America's greatest asset. Like a fine cognac his worth and value appreciates with each passing year, while the brother who's self worth is wrapped up in superficial worldly possessions slowly depreciates. The same way his useless things get old, break down or loses there shine so does he, but a Black man who doesn't determine his success by how much money is in sitting in his bank account or measure his manhood by how many women have laid in his bed, but by the content of his character, the security he's brought to his family and the glory he's given to God, this is the kind of man I'm totally in love with.

Any woman in her right mind should be head over heels in love too, posted up by her window with binoculars in hand on the lookout for a man like this to come her way. I'm not saying Black women should be like the helpless fairy tale character Rapunzel who sat in her window waiting for her knight in shining armor to come to the rescue, all I'm saying is that we need to be able to recognize the right man to let our hair down for. Too many times loneliness will sweep us down along a path of impatience that may cause us to settle for a broken down, defective substitution of love instead of holding out for the real deal. We'll plead temporary insanity because we feel there are no good Black men out there and use that as an excuse to rush into bed with or in a relationship with the first man that gives us a compliment or pays us a little attention even if he happens to be married, on drugs, criminally minded, perpetually unemployed or has absolutely no ambition, dreams, goals or reasonable plans for the future.

Backed by the sad state of affairs in our girlfriends, sisters, cousins, aunts and in our own lives we've come to the conclusion that our community is lacking available Black men with the character, honesty, integrity, respect or strength to continue on the legacy of the strong Black family that's held together the generations before us. So what have we? Forty year old women are leaving the country by the boat load trying to get their groove back, the same groove that was lost when they tied their hearts to an African American man only to have gotten burned multiple times over until they were all burnt out. Thirty year old sisters who've simply given up all hope of love with a brother are migrating towards White men, while just as hopeless twenty-somethings are deciding to have babies all by their lonesome.

For far too many beautiful Black sisters the conditions of the day are forcing us to broaden our options or straight up renegotiate our values. The brothers are out, the children are hungry, the bills are past due, the nights get lonely, what else are we going to do? In the game of life whatever's essential to survival, whatever's necessary for a somewhat bearable existence, reprieve from the mental anguish or pause from the insanity, however ugly or undesirable or broken or jagged, with open wounds, cracked feet and broken hearts that will be the road some of us choose to walk down.

When God sketched out his design for love, marriage and relationships, this meager miserable existence wasn't scribbled into his plan. God in all of His wisdom didn't intend for Black women to be in a position where we'd be forced to sacrifice our health, our morals or our sanity or our safety for companionship or a little help with the rent. God never meant for our men to be suffocated by the legal system, broken by their long standing unemployment status, or to have their spirits and bodies wrecked by drugs, alcohol and sex. The average Brother has checked out- out of our lives and out of the lives of our children, physically, emotionally and spiritually, but thank God for those above average men who are still here. The kind of men I'm in love with.

The kind of man I'm totally in love with has his keys, coat and cap still hanging onto the rack inside the home he shares with his Beautiful Black woman. Instead of running the streets he comes home early to her every night and not with the smell of cheap perfume embedded in every thread of his clothes or with a collar decorated with the faint trace of lipstick, but with love and out of respect, obligation and pure joy. His home is his castle, he is King, his woman is Queen and as royal and regal as he may be he still brings home the bacon and on occasion without pride or shame he might cook it up too. There, inside the walls of his home is a sense of security, an air of alright when he's about the place, a certain something seen in the content smile of his woman or heard in the light hearted laugh of his children. The bills are paid, the food is provided and the love overflows because daddy's home.

Instead of celebrating and supporting the extravagant lifestyle of rappers and hooraying the hustle of the hoop stars, we as Black women need to acknowledge, celebrate, encourage and uplift those above average, yet everyday brothers. Brothers who not only spend money on their kids, but brothers who spend time with their kids, brothers who aren't fleeing from commitment, but are happily bonded in marriage, brothers who legitimately work for a living, brothers who get their education on, brothers who are involved in the church and volunteer in their spare time. The ones who make it their mission to create homes and communities where the women are exalted, not beaten down, where the children are excelling instead of falling behind and where everyone knows what it feels like to be wrapped securely in love. Instead of letting these brothers go unnoticed, allowing them to slip into obscurity we aught to be lifting them up before God and thanking our gracious Lord for the sweet blessings they've showered on our community.

What we cannot afford to do is ignore their efforts, take them for granted or pretend as if what they're doing is somehow beneficial to only them and not Black people as a whole. Like the do-right brother is the norm, when in fact he is so isolated from other Black men that everyday is an uphill battle just to stay on the straight and narrow. Eight times out of ten most of his friends or so called friends are making it hard for him to live an upright life. They don't understand how he can be dedicated to just one woman, when there are hundreds of beautiful women out there who are willing to surrender all their self respect to become pawns in his and any other successful brother's pimp game. Why it's so important for him to pass on the club and stay home with his woman some nights instead of staying out until the wee hours of the morning is incomprehensible to a lot of his boys.

Some of the upright brothers friends can't fathom how he can choose to work forty or more hours in one week only to see his paycheck disappear at the end of that week after taxes, bills and savings, when he can hustle for fast money which disappears even faster on expensive electronics, flashy clothes, cheap liquor and impressing even cheaper women.

Some of these so called friends have their own values so screwed up that they're actually warped into somehow believing that the definition of manhood is being a player, hustling and basically living life selfishly without regard to other people, rules or laws. So naturally they make fun of the brother who's on the straight and narrow for being the exception, for being bold enough to use his own mind instead of following behind their misconstrued notions of life. If he sweats a little harder than the average brother because he's on the grind or if he shows any kind of above average effort, dudes at school, at work, in the neighborhood, in the locker room or on the court are starting beef with him because they think he's trying to outshine them when all he's doing is trying to better himself. The above average Black man is going to have a lot of haters.

When a Black man doesn't have another Black man patting him on the back congratulating him for his efforts or at the least encouraging him to continue on, when there's no kind of acknowledgement from his boys except negative acknowledgement that does something to his psyche. He's walking through life shipwrecked and stranded on a secluded island with none of his peers understanding where he's at or able to relate to his situation. He's feeling lost and cut off from the dominant culture that rewards a Black man for foolish behavior; cheating, lying and the like because the bar has dropped so far down the expectations for Black men are like a game of limbo, they just keep getting lower and lower.

"It's cool to treat women like trash, call them out their names, refer to yourself or your boys as niggas, do whatever for a dollar and indulge in the moment of a temporary high as opposed to planning and preparing for the future," says a morally bankrupt culture. Above average brothers have to go against the grain, work that much harder for recognition, respect and acknowledgment as they try to come up, try to do better or try to dispel the negative myths and stereotypes about themselves.

Good men have a heavy burden already placed on their backs so it's our job as women not to suffocate them, alienate them any further or force them to somehow carry the weight or pick up the slack for all the other brothers out there doing wrong. No man is a redeemer, except Jesus Christ and no man is going to save us, rescue us or erase the ugliness of our past relationships with other men. Brothers aren't meant to be messiahs, restoring our faith and hope in love and making up for the lifetime of heartache we've accrued at the hands of other brothers. This is real life, not a Tyler Perry Movie.

We shouldn't be putting that much pressure on flesh and blood human beings. When Black women start expecting Black men to patch up the holes in our hearts ripped out by other Black men, holes that only God can repair, sooner or later we'll only end up feeling empty, frustrated and disappointed because no man is equipped for soul fixing. Brothers haven't acquired some divine ability to navigate through the complicated scope of a Black woman's' mind and emotions, or dig beyond the unsightly residue of our past experiences.

Whether it's concealed by mounds of make-up, covered in accomplishments, decorated by college degrees, awards and certificates, or buried deep in our past hidden somewhere with faded pictures and old love letters, there is some kind of scar which exist deep within most Black women's soul. It might've been placed there by an absentee father, penetrated deeper by an abusive ex-boyfriend or ex-husband or ripped completely apart by our children's dad and left out raw, sore and exposed to the world, but we're hurting and we're searching for ways to manage the pain.

The tripped out thing about it is Black women have been so busy nursing our own injuries; listening to T.D. Jakes sermons religiously, reciting positive affirmations to ourselves in the mirror, reading every book by Iyanla Vanzant and other self-help gurus, pressing the rewind button like twenty times to watch and then re-watch a pissed off Bernadine burn up her cheating husband's clothes in Waiting to Exhale while smiling and saying, "That's right, git him girl," and sitting in front of the television with a pen and journal taking notes during episodes of Oprah's Lifeclass. We've spent so much time working on our issues that we didn't realize you, Black men, were hurting too, but you haven't had very may places and outlets and opportunities provided for you to appropriately handle the hurt.

We'll talk about these disappearing men and dead beat dads until we're blue in the face and as black as some of us are that's a whole lot of talking, but we don't take the time to listen to why they are gone and why they feel emotionally unattached to their children. We don't try to understand the reasoning behind their irresponsibility and apparent lack of concern for the devastating impact their behavior has on everybody, especially themselves.

Black women are guilty of sometimes being drama mama's, quick to raise our voices, quick to catch an attitude, quick to yell, scream and fight when all we need to do to begin repairing some of the rifts between our men and ourselves is shut up and stay quiet long enough to hear them out. Communication comes to a screeching halt the moment we start nagging, bickering and running our mouths. Black men press the brakes on their confessions, they shut us out, the secrets stay locked and we don't get a copy of the key because they don't want to hear our hot tempered response to whatever it is they have to say.

If we released some of the hostility we hold towards our men, cleared our hearts of resentment, maybe even worked on scrubbing away the deep rooted anger, we'd then be able to get down on our hands and knees and start praying for our men. Now is not the time to give up on Black men or get frustrated and say to hell with them. Many of us have given up already and that's understandable because we feel abandoned and we feel like Black men have given up on us, but it's not too late to come back home.

It's not too late now, but if change doesn't occur soon there will be a point in time when it will be too late; when most of our Black boys are behind bars, when not just seventy percent of our children, but all of our children are born out of wedlock because we've completely given up on marriage and decided we don't need each other for love, affection or companionship, but only for the biological functions of sex and procreation. If change doesn't occur there will be a time when the Black race no longer exists because we've completely self-destructed, but thank the Lord that time has not come yet. So now is not the time to give up. We need Black men now more than ever and the funny thing is, they need us now more than ever. We may say with our lips that we don't need you, yeah we front, but in our hearts we know we do. All the *I don't need a man* crap that we spout off is just a defense mechanism. The first sign of a hurt woman is when she opens her mouth to say, "I don't need a man," or worst is when she actually has the nerve to say she doesn't want a man. Think about it, what sane heterosexual woman actually doesn't want a man?

See brother, understand our pain and frustration and our attitudes at the end of the day when we leave our corporate jobs, jump into our expensive cars, drive to our luxurious homes which we occupy all alone and proclaim we don't need you. The warm tears shed on our empty cold bed cries out that it is a lie. Yes we need you. We need you so much that your absence is felt and deeply missed. We need you here for us physically to lead our families and to help raise our kids together. We want you here emotionally for your love and support. As a culture we depend on you spiritually, Black man, as you are the bridge between us and God. We need you alright. Most importantly from the depths of our souls to the soles of our feet we love you and we thank you, hallelujah.

Afterword

Initially this book began as an entry into a Black history month essay competition at the college I attended years ago. The rules challenged entrants to write a 1500 word or less essay about some of the issues facing the Black community in the 21st century and ways to resolve some of the problems. The hefty cash award and interesting topic motivated me to start researching, talking to people and reflecting on my own personal experiences and challenges as a Black woman as well as those around me. At the time I had no idea where it would go, if it would go anywhere and I certainly hadn't planned on it spanning further than the two and a half pages it took to write. All I knew as I began to delve head first into this subject matter, is that I had a tremendous passion for my people and the social issues and causes unique to us. I didn't win the contest, nor was I a runner up, but needless to say I gained a lot of insight into our struggles and the deep rooted sources of some of our sorrows. From this one little essay the spark had been stoked and a fire began. I wrote more and I wrote more and still I wrote more after that until a hundred and twenty-eight pages later, here you have it.

First and foremost I want to thank my Lord and Savior Jesus Christ for His saving grace and God Almighty for blessing me with the talent and the ability to do what I love and what I was created to do, which is to tell stories, teach, impart wisdom and help heal people's pain through writing. Thank you Father for the drive to persevere despite occasional bouts of fear, endless nights staring at a blank computer screen suffering from writers block and admittedly at times, self-doubt. And thank you God for the courage to touch such a sensitive topic. With regard to the personal convictions, beliefs and experiences of others I understand someone else might look at it from a completely different point of view and be highly offended by my attempt to expose some of the dirt they'd rather sweep under the rug. And just as sure as I am that some people will, I'm sure that others will nod at the truths revealed, be challenged by those same truths and appreciate seeing their own realities and feelings in print. So, to all the readers, no matter which side you fall on, thanks for taking the time to read this book. God bless you.

I'd love to hear from you

For more information about me, questions or comments contact

Lorraine Jonell Stephens

22Books

P.O. Box 17534

Sugarland, Texas 77496

Email: Info@LorraineJS.com

www.LorraineJS.com